The Peaceful Classroom in Action

Naomi Drew

♪

Jalmar Press
Torrance, California

Jalmar Press
Permissions Department
P.O. Box 1185
Torrance, CA 90505
(310) 816-3085 FAX: (310) 816-3092 e-mail: blwjalmar@worldnet.att.net

Published by Jalmar Press
THE PEACEFUL CLASSROOM IN ACTION
Author: Naomi Drew
Editor: Penworthy Learning Systems Development
Project Director: Jeanne Iler
Photographs: Bob Miller
Designer: Andrea Reider
Production: Andrea Reider
Manufactured in the United States of America
Library of Congress Number _____
First edition printing 1999: 10 9 8 7 6 5 4 3 2 1
ISBN: 1-880396-61-0

Endorsements

From Jonothan Kozol, author, *Amazing Grace* and *Savage Inequities*

"A wise and tender book; gentle, ingenious, and immensely practical. Young children can learn to navigate the channels of dissent and disagreement through these enlightened strategies. Teachers will learn from this book many proven ways to make this possible."

From Dr. Thomas Gordon, author, *Parent Effectiveness Training* and *Teacher Effectiveness Training*:

"This easy to read book will certainly provide teachers with many creative ideas, exercises, skills and materials for helping children learn peacemaking. Every teachers should have this book."

From Dr. Michele Borba, author, *Esteem Builders*:

"Naomi Drew has done it again—*The Peaceful Classroom in Action* is a gem! The simple peacemaking skills these activities teach will enhance our students emotional competence and make classrooms everywhere more caring and inviting places. I only wish every teacher could have a copy on their shelf. What a difference these peacemaking basics would make, not only in their students' live, but in our world."

From Dr. Susan Wall, Associate Director, Institute on Writing and Teaching, Northeastern University:

"How can teachers encourage young students to connect what they already know to the larger world? Naomi Drew's book addresses this question by showing how to integrate writing to teach children the personally and socially meaningful issues of peacemaking. Drawing on her own careful teacher research, she demonstrates how we can foster moral, cognitive, and literate growth."

From Gail Siggelakis, 5th grade teacher:

"Naomi Drew's book *Learning the Skills of Peacemaking* is the foundation for all I do with my students. *The Peaceful Classroom in Action* is its perfect compliment. It will help teachers more fully infuse peacemaking into the life of the classroom. This book is so readable and insightful, you won't want to put it down. Naomi does for peacemaking what Lucy Calkings has done for the writing process."

From Tobi Gerard, Kindergarten teacher:

"Since using Naomi Drew's *Learning the Skills of Peacemaking*, I've noticed my students talking out problems, listening to each other, and showing more care. I have seen a transformation even in children this young. The Peaceful Classroom in Action is the next step to help teachers develop an atmosphere of peace and compassion in the classroom. What a treasure! This is one resource that will never be far from your side. Thanks, Naomi."

From Lois Samelson, First grade teacher:

"*The Peaceful Classroom in Action* is inspiring, practical, and highly usable. It will surely impact my teaching on a daily basis, and has the potential to change the lives of my students. It's a must-read for all elementary teachers and administrators."

From Dr. Lois Braender, Principal:

"Just as education is the cornerstone of nonviolent living, Naomi Drew's first book *Learning the Skills of Peacemaking* became the cornerstone of our school-wide conflict resolution program. Our efforts earned a Best Practice Award and a Star School Award. In addition, we received a Goals 2000 Grant to expand conflict resolution throughout our school district using Naomi Drew's ideas. I am excited at the prospect of implementing *The Peaceful Classroom in Action* and am delighted that Naomi Drew has now infused conflict resolution into language arts.

From Michiko Kuroda, United Nations:

This book demonstrates how children can learn and apply peacemaking skills in their daily lives and grow at the same time. I believe only through hands-on experiences can children effectively learn peacemaking, from which classmates, teachers, parents and everybody else will benefit. This book also provides very rich materials and references that the readers can always go back to. This is definitely a valuable contribution to peacemaking in our communities, our nation(s) and even in the world. It is Naomi Drew's love of children, dedication to work on conflict resolution and sincere desire for peace in the world that made it possible to complete such a voluminous work. Those who will feel her energy throughout the book must be on the path to peacemaking and peace in the world."

Acknowledgements

We never truly write alone. Our thoughts generate from remembered (and sometimes forgotten) conversations, stored bits of information culled from varied sources, and insights gained from living and learning. We exist in an intertextual universe enriched by the perceptions of others. No book is ever conceived solely by one person. I am indebted to many.

My deepest gratitude to my many wonderful instructors and colleagues in the Martha's Vineyard Summer Institute on Writing and Teaching sponsored by Northeastern University, particularly Susan Wall and Glenda Bissex. Their expert guidance and support helped make this book possible. Their keen insights made it richer.

To my dear friends Gail Siggelakis and Carol Lyons, I offer love and thanks for their insights and help; but moreover, for the continuous faith in me they so readily express.

To my writing-support colleague, Gail Cassidy, I express deep gratitude for two years of Wednesday night phone calls that often provided my greatest impetus to keep on writing.

To my editors at Penworthy, Tamera Bryant and Dorinda Clippinger, and to Jeanne Iler at Jalmar Press, my gratitude for their support and professionalism.

To Bob Miller for taking all of the photographs in this book.

To Kathy Patton and Camille Maxwell my warmest thanks for their valuable feedback on the manuscript of this book.

To all of the children in my 1995-96 and 1996-97 second grade classes at the Cambridge School in South Brunswick, New Jersey, whose words and deeds created the core of this book, I extend my love, gratitude, and respect. I will always remember you.

To my wonderful husband and sons, I express my greatest debt of gratitude for their deep, unconditional love and constant support, and for the enduring sense of happiness they provide for me.

Second only to what happens between parent and
child what happens in the classroom determines the
shape of culture and evolution of consciousness.

Mary Rose O'Reilley
The Peaceable Classroom

This book is dedicated to the memory of my mother
Molly Schreiber
whose humanitarian values and deep respect for all people form its core.
My mother's teachings have been my greatest source of inspiration.
May her beliefs touch the hearts and shape the actions of people throughout this world.

Table of Contents

The purpose of education is to create a higher sense of the possible.
Norman Cousins, Human Options, 29

Appendix

Your At-A Glance Guide to Key Peacemaking Processes in this Book

Creating a Peaceful Classroom (Description: page 5; Lesson: Page 115)

In this section you will discover how to introduce peacemaking on the first day of school, laying a framework that will last all year long. "Our Peace Pledge" is included in this section.

Giving "I messages" (Description: page 14; Lesson: page 123)

"I messages" are simple declarative statements starting with "I" that express one's needs, concerns, or feelings. Find out how to teach and use this key element of effective communication and conflict resolution.

Introducing The Win/Win Guidelines (Description: page 14; Lessons: page 119 and 121)

This six-step strategy will help your students (and you) resolve conflicts successfully. Thoroughly field-tested and used internationally, the Win/Win Guidelines are an effective method for communication in conflicts of any kind.

Fostering Good Listening Skills (Description: page 23; Lesson: page 139)

Good listening is the basis for all effective communication. Listening enables children to learn better, have healthier relationships, and resolve conflicts. Find out how to teach these invaluable skills in this section.

Showcasing Conflict Resolution (Description: page 29)

Showcasing means mediating selected conflicts in front of the entire class to help kids gain practice in conflict resolution. See how showcasing is incorporated into a classroom setting.

How and When to Mediate (Description: page 31)

Learn what you need to do to mediate a conflict your students are engaged in. Find out when you should step in.

Calmness in the Classroom (Description: page 57)

Learn some simple but highly effective techniques that will help you and your students feel calm in and out of the classroom.

Integrating Writing and Peacemaking (Description: page 61)

Improve your children's writing as they learn to be peacemakers when you combine the writing process and peacemaking skills. Find out how.

Integrating Literature and Peacemaking (Description and lessons: page 87)

Eleven new lessons will help you motivate and reinforce peacemaking skills through works of fiction, nonfiction, and poetry.

Eleven Peacemaking Lessons at Your Fingertips: (page 115)

Lessons on conflict resolution, self-esteem, acceptance of differences, and others are included in this section.

Pacing Yourself

Before School Starts

- Set up a Work-it-Out spot in you classroom (Chapter 2, page 12).
- Hang "Peacemaker of The Week" bulletin board (page 41).
- Hang "Our Peace Pledge" (page 5).
- Practice "Breathing for Calmness" (page 5).
- Practice using "I messages" in your own life (page 14).
- Practice using the Win/Win Guidelines when you have a conflict (page 14).
- Choose at least two calmness techniques to do daily (page 53–58).
- Buy some tapes with quiet music to keep in your classroom. Choose tapes you can play as background music when the children are writing. Select some peacemaking tapes recommended in the appendix.

The First Weeks of School

- Lesson: Creating a Peaceful Classroom (page 115).
- Lesson: "I messages" (page 123).
- Lesson: Resolving Conflicts: The Quick Method (page 119 or 124).
- Lesson: The Process of Affirming (page 127).
- Lesson: Reflective Listening with Conflicts (page 139).
- Story: *The Secret of the Peaceful Warrior* (page 4).

Processes to do Every Day all Year

- Morning Peace Pledge (page 4).
- Breathing for Calmness (page 58).
- Make sure students honor your Guidelines for a Peaceful Classroom (page 5–8).
- Catch your students in the act of doing things right.
- Help students mediate their conflicts using Win/Win Guidelines (page 29, 31).
- Reinforce good listening skills (page 23).
- Quiet writing time. Start each day with this.

Processes to do at Least Every Week or Two All Year

- Review your Guidelines for a Peaceful Classroom (page 7).
- Review chart, "A Peacemaker is Someone Who. . . ." (page 12).
- Peacemaker of the Week (page 41).
- Follow up morning Peace Pledge by having students give examples of how they are being peacemakers (page 4). NOTE: Do the Peace Pledge daily at beginning of year.
- Peacemaking Journals (page 41).
- Peacemaking-related stories (resource section).
- Cooperative group activities (example: page 37–41).

Call To Action

I know of no safe depository of the ultimate powers of society but the people themselves, and, if we think them not enlightened enough to exercise their control with a wholesome direction, the remedy is not to take it from them, but to inform their discretion by education.

Thomas Jefferson

What gives hope its power is not the accumulation of demonstrable facts, but the release of human energies generated by the longing for something better.

Norman Cousins, p. 57

Teachers have the power to shape lives. More than members of any other profession, teachers have the ability to affect the future— a tremendous honor and responsibility.

Do you realize that as teachers we spend more time with students than many of their parents do? Teachers provide children with life-altering skills and make a staggering impact. Now we must rise to the call of another need—the need for new basic skills that will help children survive into the third millennium.

Our country is reeling from an increase in violence that affects all communities, large and small, urban and suburban, rich and poor. In his groundbreaking book *Emotional Intelligence*, Daniel Goleman wrote, "As a society we have not bothered to make sure every child is taught the essentials of handling anger or resolving conflict positively—nor have we bothered to teach empathy, impulse control, or any of the other fundamentals of emotional competence" (286). Clearly, unless we teach children how to get along, everyone's future will be at risk.

The good news, however, is this: Things are slowly beginning to change. Teenagers in the South Bronx are learning to resolve differences nonviolently; kindergarten children in the suburbs are speaking "I messages"; and parents who attend peacemaking workshops are reinforcing peacemaking skills at home. More and more people are asking that peace and acceptance be taught in schools, not as an add-on to the curriculum, but as the foundation for success in all areas. In the words of Roger and David Johnson, "Teachers cannot teach and students cannot learn unless there is peace and order in the classroom."

Stephen O'Connor, author of *Will My Name Be Shouted Out*, said, "The single factor that most frustrates any teacher in reaching his or her goals is the relentless intrusion of social problems into the classroom" (Ayers, 23). Teachers can do little to rectify the devastating home lives many children endure; but we can provide another reality when children are in school, creating an environment where they feel safe, accepted, nurtured, and respected. In this environment children can be taught alternatives to the violence that surrounds all of us, helping them perceive hopeful options for their futures.

How do we begin? A hard question. I believe we have to start with the basics, but at this time, the "basics" are not what they used to be. The changing texture of our complex and violent society has given way to the need for what I call "the new basics," without which children will have little chance of succeeding socially, emotionally, or academically. And what elements can we designate as the new basics? I suggest the following:

The New Basics: What Children Need to Succeed

- sense of hope
- respect for self and others
- positive self-image
- the ability to work cooperatively
- a sense of empathy toward others
- anger management skills
- firm but fair consistent limits
- strategies for resolving conflicts nonviolently
- a sense of personal responsibility for one's behavior
- the knowledge that our actions make a difference to the world around us
- an understanding that violence in any form is not acceptable

How can teachers give these basics to children? By bringing peace education to every child in every classroom in every school throughout the country. You may ask, "What about parent involvement and community efforts to change things? The schools can't do it all." You're right, the schools can't do it all; but by teaching the skills of peacemaking teachers will take a crucial role in shaping America's future.

Is the order too tall? Is it too late? Have things gotten so far out of hand they've become hopeless? I think not. Norman Cousins once said, "The starting point for a better world is the belief that it is possible" (*Human Options*, 51). As educators, we need much to believe that our children *can* have a better world, and that change *is* possible. And whom does a better world start with? It starts with each of us.

The future of this society may well rest in the hands of teachers. We need to do whatever we can to reshape the current course of violence and divisiveness in our children's futures, one moment at a time, one child at a time. Can we do it? I believe we can, one teacher at a time.

Using This Book

Human existence cannot be silent, nor can it be nourished by false words, but only true words, with which men and women transform the world.

Paulo Friere, 69

The work of transformation goes on at many levels: in the halls of government, in the framing of public policy, in the minds of poets, in the eyes of artists, and in the classroom where we teach. Teaching is by nature a transforming experience. By schooling the minds of children we shape the future.

It is my hope that this book will be another tool for transformation, enabling you to bring new skills, concepts, and understandings into your classroom. And as you do so, share what you discover with colleagues. Don't allow new insights to remain within the walls of your own room. Encourage yourself to be another conduit for change, bringing new understandings to the parents of your students, your professional colleagues, your administrators, and your community. What takes place in your classroom can provide scaffolding for people who are uninitiated into the skills of peacemaking. Open your doors; share what you learn.

This book has been designed to support you in teaching and sharing many different peacemaking skills. The classroom anecdotes and strategies described on these pages will enable you to begin creating a peaceful classroom from the first day of school, extending it throughout the entire year. And the research woven through each chapter will give you plenty of data to share with those who may need convincing that peacemaking should be a key component of the curriculum.

Although most of the students described in *The Peaceful Classroom in Action* are second graders, much of the material in this book has been used in elementary classrooms throughout the United States and other countries, from kindergarten through sixth grade, in regular classes as well as special education, in urban as well as suburban schools. It is highly adaptable and intended to be modified for your particular age group. So feel free to reshape these strategies and make them your own. If you believe a certain activity won't work with your group, change it to fit the needs of your students, your grade level. Remember, this book is about change; so try to embrace the process of change as you use it.

NOTE: If you haven't already read *Learning the Skills of Peacemaking* from the same author and publisher, you are encouraged to do so. It will give you a solid foundation for the teaching of peacemaking and will provide many lessons to supplement the ones in this book.

The Peaceful Classroom in Action is in three sections:

Part I   Creating a Peaceful Classroom
Part II   Integrating Writing and Peacemaking
Part III Integrating Literature and
          Peacemaking: A Primary Unit

Children's literature is used extensively in each section of this book. Many of the lessons you are about to read incorporate children's books that elucidate and reinforce peacemaking concepts. Children identify with story characters, empathizing, solving problems, perceiving outcomes, and vicariously putting into practice their knowledge of peacemaking skills. Each time children help a story character resolve a conflict, they engage in a form of mental rehearsal for similar situations that may arise in their own lives. Stories also help children deal with emotional issues that may hamper positive relationships. You'll see how literature is used to inform, support, and enlighten children on many levels.

Part I, Creating a Peaceful Classroom, shows specifically how to bring peacemaking into your classroom at the beginning of the year and how to integrate, reinforce and extend it as the year goes on. Particular attention is given to the first month of school, the time when the foundation is set. Among the many lessons and anecdotes in this section are "Creating a Peaceful Classroom," "Introducing the Win/Win Guidelines," and "Showcasing Conflict Resolution," initially presented in *Learning the Skills of Peacemaking*. For your convenience, copies of the original lessons appear in the Appendix.

You will also find examples of children applying peacemaking skills and understandings as they learn math, science, and reading. Many of these anecdotes highlight collaborative learning, which fosters key elements of the peacemaking process: sharing, negotiating, empathizing and compromising.

Part II, Integrating Writing and Peacemaking, highlights the link between these areas, showing how one process reinforces and supports the other. How to integrate the two is illustrated through the writing samples and conversations of my second grade students, showing how they developed both as writers and peacemakers.

All activities in this section are easily adaptable to various grade levels.

Among the topics the children speak and write about are, "How I am a Peacemaker," "Dealing with Prejudice," "Working Out Conflicts," and "Why Peacemaking is Important."

Part III, Integrating Literature and Peacemaking: A Primary Unit, contains eleven lessons that reinforce key peacemaking concepts including caring for the world around us, solving problems, accepting differences, taking personal responsibility for one's actions, confronting racism, and resolving conflicts. A variety of literature is used, ranging from fiction to poetry to biography. The unit culminates in a Peace Day Celebration, a multifaceted activity that pulls together the overarching concepts taught throughout the unit.

Lessons 5, 8, 9, 10, and 11 of the unit are appropriate for the upper elementary grades as well as primary grades. In the Appendix, are six lessons *from Learning the Skills of Peacemaking* and five new lessons that relate to content throughout the book. Many of these lessons are appropriate for Grades 2 through 6, and several can be used at all grade levels. Each lesson in the Appendix shows at the top of the page the grade levels it's intended for.

"When will I ever find time to teach more lessons?" you may be asking yourself right now (as I do whenever I hear about something new to teach). You will find that you can easily integrate lessons in this book into your weekly schedules. I always regard peacemaking as my social studies unit for the fall. Many teachers use peacemaking as their language arts lesson for the day. Each lesson has been designed to tie in to objectives in either social studies, language arts, or health (self-esteem, communication, getting along with others.) I suggest that you start the year with lessons in the Appendix (pp. 115–149), beginning with "Creating a Peaceful Classroom" and then following the sequence of lessons as they are arranged. Save the Primary Unit for mid-year as a means of reinforcement. *Most importantly, be sure to think, act, and speak peacemaking every day of the school year. Your being a living model is the most powerful way to make peacemaking come alive for your students.*

As you use this book, go back and forth between the sections, interweaving concepts and strategies. The "Pacing Yourself" section (xii) will help you do this. Also, on page xv is an At-A-Glance Guide to the Key Peacemaking Concepts in This Book designed for your easy reference.

There is a little gift for you in Part I. It's a chapter called "Taking Care of Ourselves." Teaching peacemaking to children starts with each of us. We teach peace effectively only when we have the actual experience of it in our own lives. After all, we are the people our children look to for validation of the ideals and concepts we bring to them.

Through this chapter you will discover techniques and insights that can bring greater peace to your life. It's a huge challenge to live with all the demands of a teaching career and family and still find a way to feel peaceful inside. Teachers not only deal with the ever-growing pressures of work; we also have homes, children, bills, laundry, food shopping, and a multitude of other responsibilities that must be constantly juggled. This chapter will enable you to create a greater sense of harmony, balance, and well-being in spite of all the pressures. As you read it, put up your feet and relax, and be sure to do something nurturing for yourself before the day ends.

May *The Peaceful Classroom in Action* bring positive changes to you, to your students, to your school, and and to the world at large. Peace to all of you.

Introduction

A teacher affects eternity; he can never tell where his influence stops.

(Henry Adams)

Peace is a never-ending process that demands constant attention and absolute commitment, but the rewards are great.

(Starting Small, 145)

Since writing *Learning the Skills of Peacemaking,* I have returned to the classroom and have been teaching peacemaking to children and leading workshops for educators and parents. Along with insights gained from the many workshop participants I have met around the country, my students have been my most valuable teachers. They've led me to a deeper understanding of the application of peacemaking skills to many aspects of living and learning. Through this book I share my understandings of these applications, extending an invitation for you to step into my classroom through the pages of my journal and see how these skills are applied across the curriculum.

In *Learning the Skills of Peacemaking,* peacemaking skills are defined as follows:

- acceptance of self and others
- demonstration of respect for others
- cooperation
- conflict resolution
- personal responsibility for one's actions
- a sense of connection to and responsibility toward the larger world

The original 1985 field study for *Learning the Skills of Peacemaking* showed not only that children can learn to resolve conflicts, but also that when they do so, their self-esteem increases.

Since my return to teaching, I have felt the need to observe children more closely, noting subtle changes in them when peacemaking is woven into the fabric of each day. I have seen that the hearts of young children, not yet hardened by the ways of the world, are open and ready to absorb lessons in peace. There is little to unlearn when a child is young.

Over the past two years I have closely watched my students in the process of learning and socializing, following them around with my journal as they engaged in math, reading, language arts, social studies, and science activities, and participated in collaborative projects. During school I would quickly jot down the children's conversations, noting the way they interacted with one another, and at the end of the day, when the room was finally quiet, I would sit at my desk digesting the notes I had taken, reflecting on what I had seen. Through this book I ask you to join me in the classroom seeing what I saw, learning what I learned.

A source of deep insight was the children's writing, which revealed much about their thoughts, feelings, and attitudes. *In Social Worlds of Children Learning to Write,* Anne Haas Dyson said, ". . .the intertextual universe of the classroom itself attains sociocultural depth, as diverse genres, diverse cultural traditions, mingle on the classroom stage, giving rise to new possibilities, new speculations, new styles" (216). Dyson believed that when children are given the freedom to express themselves in language that is fully their own, a sociocultural depth comes to the classroom and possibilities for even greater self-expression emerge. In the safe environment of our peaceful classroom, children's minds thrived, hearts opened, and words flowed. Part II of this book focuses on this process and the clear link between writing and peacemaking.

My colleagues were enormously helpful to me in formulating new insights. Often, our conversations would deepen my awareness and help me gain new perceptions that might not have otherwise crystalized. In *The Art of Classroom Inquiry* Lee Odell said, "Exploration leads to further exploration, discovery to still further discovery" (Hubbard, *Power* xv). New understandings developed and new questions took shape through interactions with colleagues. As you begin to teach the skills of peacemaking, partner with a colleague who also is teaching peacemaking. You'll need to support each other as you journey through some unfamiliar terrain, exploring questions, discussing problems, and sharing successes. It's always better to travel a new path with a trusted partner.

Through my own process of continued observation, reflection, and sharing, I came to know my students of the past two years far better than any I'd taught in the previous eighteen years. The children you will meet in this book are representative of many others across the country, being of varied ethnic, sociocultural, and economic backgrounds, with a wide variety of learning abilities and differing family backgrounds. Many of my students had emotional challenges that surfaced through their writing and conversations; their courage to open up was a contribution to the tenor of the class. The safety, acceptance, and compassion of the peaceful classroom made their deep sharing possible.

As you teach peacemaking to your students, living these skills and attitudes in your own life is essential. By doing so, you will be far better able to model what you teach authentically—and authenticity is key. We need to teach children to do what we do, not just what we say.

It's also important to weave the skills and concepts of peacemaking into other areas of the curriculum as a process and as a vehicle for learning. When we do so, our students grow socially and emotionally, as well as academically. As the peaceful classroom takes root and grows, we begin to see that its homeostasis is achieved by each person's continuous investment in the well-being of others. A growing sense of interdependence then begins to flourish. The learning community is firmly established as a growing dynamic organism. Change takes root.

The process of peacemaking is exactly that—process. This book is not a simple "how-to," promising a peaceful classroom in thirty days if you follow its directions. The true meaning of this book will only be revealed to you as you live the concepts within it. To explain better what I mean, I must share the words of one of my editors, Tamera Bryant, who so beautifully framed her deep understanding of this idea in a letter to me:

> . . . the peaceful classroom is never a product, certainly not a finished product. It's a living, breathing organism that's always evolving and changing with each glimpse or grasping of a new insight or a deepened understanding.

No one can read this book simply for information. Although it's filled with facts, none of them working alone will help, The only way to learn from this book is to practice it. The only way to believe it is to do it. The only way to feel its effects is to live it. When teachers do that, this book will take on a whole new life. Layers of meaning will pile up everywhere.

May this book enable greater numbers of us to live the skills of peacemaking, and in doing so, imbue our students with its essence, so that together we may contribute the possibility of peace for all people.

PART *One*

Creating
a Peaceful
Classroom

It Starts with You

Let the eyes
inside your heart
see into the hearts
of others.

Realize
they have the need
to be accepted
just like you.

Let them see you care,
open up your mind,
treat them with respect,
show that you're a friend.

When you do this
you will find
others treating
you the same,

opening their eyes
to look inside your heart
returning the respect
you have given them.

And one by one
the world will change;
a brighter sun
will start to rise

reminding us
that peace for all
is rooted in
the things we do.

—*Naomi Drew*

"What do you mean, 'different on the outside'?" asked Terrence.

A perfect entree into the issue of diversity, I thought. "Terrence, your skin is brown and my skin is tan. I'm a female and you're a male; I'm big and you're little. We're different on the outside. But we're both human beings, and we both have feelings. We want the same things: to be treated with kindness and respect, right?"

"Right," said Terrence "Hey, Arjay has gold skin."

"I have brown skin like you," Billy said, turning to Terrence.

"I have pinkish skin with freckles," Allison joined in. Soon the children were holding up their arms and comparing each other's skin tones, then hair colors, eye colors, and heights. After the discussion went on awhile, I said, "Sometimes when people don't know about peacemaking, they treat others in a mean way because they're different on the outside."

"That's crazy," said Amanda, " 'cause inside we're really the same."

"It **is** crazy, Amanda," I said, "but sometimes people need to be reminded that we're all the same inside. By your remembering it, you can set a positive example for others in and out of school."

"What else did you think about when you pictured having a peaceful classroom ?"

The children's hands shot up, and they talked about the many qualities they had imagined a peaceful classroom would have. As they spoke, I listed each quality on a chart, as shown below.

A Peaceful Classroom Looks Like This

- People are kind to each other.
- We don't use put-downs.
- People speak in kind voices, not yelling voices.
- People don't hurt each other.
- People care about each other.
- We use our manners.
- We feel safe here.

"What about if people get into conflicts?" I asked.

"What's a conflict; I forgot?" asked Justin.

I wrote the word "conflict" on the board and repeated what I had said during the reading of *The Secret of the Peaceful Warrior*. "A conflict is a fight or disagreement. People get into conflicts all the time; it's just part of being human. The thing that's bad about conflicts is that people often don't handle them in a peaceful way. A lot of people hit, or yell, or call one another names when involved in a conflict. What else can you do if you get into a conflict?"

"Talk it out," said Amanda.

"Use your words and not your fists," added Caitlin.

"Ask for help," said Hannah.

"That's right!" I said adding to our chart, "People work out conflicts using their words."

After completing the list of qualities, I said, "Now, let's think of some guidelines we can follow every day so we can have a peaceful classroom throughout the year." The children and I looked at the chart we had just created, this time thinking about the steps each person could take to make a peaceful classroom a reality. Gradually, this list emerged.

To Have a Peaceful Classroom

We Agree To Do the Following:

- Treat each other with kindness and respect.
- Not fight.
- Work out our conflicts with words, not fists.
- Stop conflicts before they even start
- Respect each other's things.
- Include each other when we play.
- Share.
- Not use put-downs.
- Always remember that we are all the same inside even if we **look different on the outside.**

When the chart of guidelines was complete, I asked the children if they'd each commit to being responsible for abiding by these guidelines. We talked about the meaning of responsibility and how each person makes a difference in the tenor of a class. I then asked every child to sign the chart, calling it "our contract." I added, "When you sign a contract, you are giving your word of honor that you will do everything in your power to follow what we agreed to. Do you think you can do that?" One by one each child stepped forward, picked up a colored marker and signed the contract.

I laminated the guidelines and displayed them in the most prominent place in the room, reviewing them frequently and introducing them to each new child who entered the class. The children's parents were introduced to our guidelines on Back-To-School Night.

Reflections

We covered a lot of ground in this lesson, focusing on qualities that foster a peaceful classroom, then looking at the issue of personal responsibility, acceptance of differences, and the importance of working out conflicts. The idea I brought home again and again was: A peaceful classroom is one in which people feel safe, respected, and cared for. Perhaps more important to the children was the overriding message that their input was crucial to the creation of a peaceful classroom.

This lesson was one of many early steps toward building an "atmosphere of thinking, discussing, and problem solving" that William Glasser referred to in *Schools Without Failure*. He believed this kind of atmosphere leads children to be more independent and socially adept, saying, "Children can learn that their peers care about them. They learn to solve the problems of their world" (131). Imagine the implications for the future.

Along with many teachers across the country, I have found this particular lesson to be highly effective in setting the tone for a peaceful classroom throughout the year. As one teacher said, "When you involve the children right from the start, it's different from just giving them rules. You engage their thinking and allow them to take greater ownership. That's why this strategy works."

Insights on the First Day of School

Flannery O'Connor said, "A story is a way to say something that can't be said any other way." Stories have the power to lead us toward knowledge and insight. For this reason I chose to introduce peacemaking concepts through a story rather than a didactic discussion. *The Secret of the Peaceful Warrior* has strong enough characterization and narrative to sweep the children into Danny's plight, enabling them to identify with his problem and share in the satisfaction of his solution.

The philosopher Jacques Barzun talked about the power of stories: "The best literature . . . carries us back to reality" (qtd. in Kilpatrick, 137). This concept is extended in the book *Why Johnny Can't Tell Right From Wrong*, which assures us that good literature helps develop morality.

> It involves us in the detail and particularity of other lives. And unlike the superficial encounters of the workaday world, a book shows us what other lives are like from the inside. Moral principles also take on a reality in stories that they lack in purely logical form. Stories restrain our tendency to indulge in abstract speculation about ethics. They make it a little harder for us to reduce people to factors in an equation. (137)

The children's strong identification with Danny helped them assimilate the same lessons in peacemaking that Danny did. Danny's plight became their own, as did his newly found insights. Literature is a powerful tool for teaching values to children. This topic is discussed further in Part III.

The Secret of the Peaceful Warrior was one of many vehicles used to suffuse my class with peacemaking on the first day of school. My purpose for such intense coverage was threefold:

- I wanted to build a scaffold for excellent behavior.
- I wanted to lay the groundwork for academic achievement by creating an atmosphere of trust, respect, and calmness.
- I wanted to create a framework for the children's thinking that included the following beliefs:
  - Class is built on mutual respect.
  - People can make positive choices in the face of conflict.
  - Fighting is not one of the better choices.
  - Each person is special and worthy of being treated with dignity.
  - Our actions make a difference.

The transformational work of peacemaking now begun, we can look ahead to a year of enhanced learning and better relationships. We can look to the future and see possibility.

Research on the Academic Impact of Peacemaking

The process of peacemaking has the potential to affect children's academic performance. Roger Johnson and David Johnson have done extensive research on peacemaking and its effect on children's learning and behavior, finding that when we teach our children how to get along, accept differences, and resolve conflicts, they learn better. Roger Johnson (1992) introduced this idea in *Educational Leadership*: "Students who know how to manage their own behavior have a developmental advantage over those who don't" (11).

Johnson and Johnson conducted the most comprehensive study to date on how peacemaking influences children's attitudes, behaviors, and academic achievement. In *Conflict Resolution and Peer Mediation Programs in Elementary and Secondary Schools: A Review of the Research*, the researchers cited various studies supporting their 1992 claim. In fact, in a 1995 study co-conducted with Stevahn and Real, Johnson and Johnson found a link between academic achievement and the teaching of peacemaking (specifically, conflict resolution and cooperative learning). In that study, seventh and eighth graders were assigned to cooperative groups where they learned conflict resolution skills prior to the administration of an achievement test. This group was compared to other seventh and eighth graders who had either no training or less comprehensive taining. "The highest achievements on both a posttest and a retention test were found in the cooperative learning/conflict training condition . . . " (47). Johnson and Johnson also found a link between integrating the teaching of peacemaking skills in subject areas and increased achievement, which is encouraging. "There is also evidence that the integration and the learning of the conflict resolution and peer mediation procedures can increase students' academic achievement " (46). Conversely, a study by Berndt and Keefe (1992) showed that "increases in conflict between friends longitudinally predict detachment from school and lower grades" (46). From three separate studies Johnson and Johnson concluded that conflict resolution integrated into academic units and combined with cooperative learning can increase achievement. (47)

While I am encouraged by these findings, I am not surprised. Without exception, during my twenty years of teaching, I have found that peacemaking enhances the arena for learning. It happens for two main reasons. The first reason: More time is freed up for teaching, and less time is spent on discipline. Incidences of conflict diminish, positive peer relationships thrive, and an atmosphere of safety develops. Then, the second reason: Children learn better in an atmosphere of safety. When they feel safe, supported, and accepted they can focus better on the task of learning. Unencumbered by petty conflicts and the hostility of others, children can engage in learning as a joyful process, one that's vital, exciting, alive.

Think about yourself. Don't you function better when you're among friendly, caring, accepting people? Imagine creating an atmosphere in your classroom where this is the standard. How much more learning could take place! Remember, as well, that we are shaping minds not only so that children can succeed in school but so that they can succeed in *life*.

CHAPTER Two

The First Week of School

While schools teach math, reading, social studies, and science, perhaps the most important thing for students to learn is how to interact effectively and peacefully with each other and the world at large.

—Roger Johnson and David Johnson, Peacemakers, 1:1

The vision of community that the classroom provides can color a child's ideas and expectations about equity, cooperation and citizenship for a lifetime.

—Jim Carnes, Starting Small, v

Creating a Caring Environment

Environmental factors are very important in creating a peaceful classroom. The posters, visuals, and bulletin boards that adorn your walls; the way furniture is arranged (Is it conducive to group interaction and shared learning?); accessibility of materials to the children; brightness and color—all of these help set the tone. In this chapter you're invited into my classroom (entering through the pages of my journal) to see how the physical environment is created. Next we'll look at a lesson introducing the Win/Win Guidelines through puppets. Lastly, we'll talk about the importance of setting ethical standards, having high expectations, offering affirmation, and fostering good listening skills as foundational elements of the peaceful classroom.

Journal Entry: September. 10, 8:45 A.M.

The first day of school passed quickly! One student commented that it felt good to be in our classroom. I realize that aside from the peacemaking activities, the physical space of this room is inviting. I look around at the three parallel tables at the center of the room and the bright yellow name tags decorated with stickers. There's plenty of space at the front and back of the room for the children to sit on the carpet for class discussions and cooperative groups. Every wall is covered with signs, pictures, posters, and quotations. Wanting to make the children feel special right away, I hung this poem on the easel to read with them over and over.

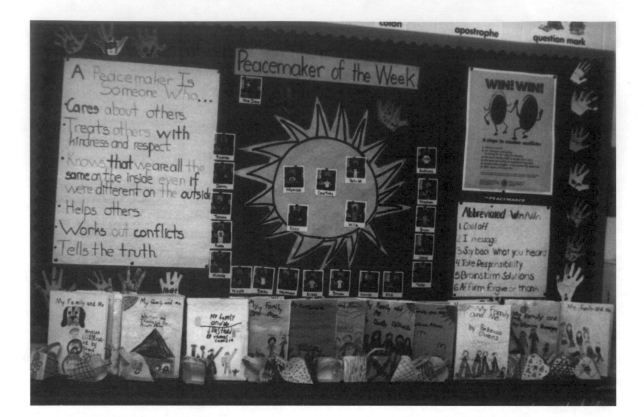

Being Human is Being Special

I look in the mirror,

and who do I see?
My very own person
who looks just like me!
I look at my eyes,
I look at my face,
knowing that no one
on earth or in space,
is quite like I am,
one of a kind.
My body is special
and so is my mind.

Each person alive
has something special to give.
We each make a difference
each day that we live.
I love myself,
and I love others too.
The world is a special place
'cause it has me and you.

—Drew, 67

On the front chalkboard is a large chart on which I drew a giant heart for the children to write their names on. At the top of the paper are the words, "Welcome, My Peacemakers." One of the children gave me that idea. Wanting to get the students motivated over the summer, I wrote a letter to all of them expressing my excitement about their coming to second grade, and my own experiences when I started second grade at age seven. I also invited some of the children who lived near the school to come in and help set up the room. Mary Lynn and Alyssia were able to come, and Mary Lynn asked if she could bring Chris (her big brother) and Sheena (her big sister). Alyssia brought her little sister (Amanda) as well.

We worked together setting up interest centers in the room: blocks, math, science, reading, and computers. After working with the younger children and me for three days, Sheena came in with a stack of bulletin board ideas, all related to peacemaking. "Mrs. Drew, here are some ideas to get the year started. I hope you like them," she said expectantly. Her "Welcome, My Peacemakers" idea was the best.

The kids also helped hang our Peacemaker of the Week bulletin board (Drew, 113) at the back of the room. This display will stay up all year, a permanent acknowledgement of the children's best efforts at peacemaking. Today I'm going to take snapshots of everyone in the class to put around the perimeter of the bulletin board. On alternating Fridays we—the children and I—will select those students who've most consistently exhibited peacemaking qualities, and their pictures will go in a large yellow "sunshine" at the center of this bulletin board. What qualities are we looking for? Qualities are listed on a chart to the left of the photographs.

A Peacemaker Is Someone Who . . .

- Cares about others.
- Treats people with kindness and respect
- Helps others.
- Works out conflicts without fighting.
- Is a good listener.
- Tells the truth.
- Knows that people are the same on the inside even if we look different on the outside.

On the right of the children's pictures are the Win/Win Guidelines, a six-step strategy for resolving conflicts (see page 0). I'll introduce the Win/Win Guidelines this morning so the children will know how to work out conflicts right away.

In the back corner where our classroom library is set up, there's a small white table with green chairs. A teddy bear sits in one of those chairs, always ready to give up the seat to a child with a problem to negotiate. This is our "Work-it-out Spot," a place where any child can sit down to resolve problems with a peer. Another copy of the Win/Win Guidelines is posted in this corner, with the intention that many conflicts will be resolved here.

The kids will come in soon. Let's see, what do I most want to focus on today? Respect, creating good listening skills, and acknowledgment of positive behaviors. Also, fun, can't forget about fun. I want them to love being here, and I want to feel the same way .

Reflections

How deliberate we have to be about moving toward our goal of creating a peaceful classroom; it doesn't just happen of its own accord. In *Teaching Tolerance* magazine, one elementary teacher, said, "We can't just assume children know how to work together. Cooperative skills are something we have to teach" (59). In the twenty years that I've taught I have found that statement to be true. Like all human beings, our children have within them the seeds of peace. It's up to us, their teachers and parents to nurture those seeds and help them grow. Creating a caring learning environment through the physical elements of a classroom is an important part of this process.

What if you have extremely limited space? Fear not, you can still adorn your walls with peacemaking-related posters, pictures and quotations. On a limited budget? Have your students create their own drawings, posters, and poems. Find related quotations in this book and others. Copy them onto large paper and have your students decorate them. The most important thing is that your room, no matter how large or small, reflect care, acceptance, and harmony. It should be a welcoming place that also feels safe and stimulating to children. Most of all, it should feel peaceful. Ask yourself this question: "Does my room give me a feeling of peacefulness and excitement for learning when I walk in?" If the answer is no, make some changes. When a teacher I know decided to decorate each station in her computer lab with posters, stuffed animals, and figurines, her room came alive. What can you do to make your room the warmest, most welcoming place imaginable?

Introducing the Win/Win Guidelines

. . . there are impartial, fair ways to settle pint-size disputes, while the deeper teaching is that disputes can be negotiated. (Daniel Goleman, 272)

The Win/Win Guidelines

1. Take time to cool off.
2. Each person gives an "I message," stating feelings about a problem. No put-downs, blaming or name-calling.
3. Each person states the problem as the other person sees it, reflecting what they have heard.
4. Each person takes responsibility for his or her role in the problem.
5. Brainstorm solutions together, and choose a solution that satisfies both people, a win/win solution.
6. Affirm, forgive, or thank each other.
   (Drew, 77)

This strategy is currently used in elementary, middle, and high schools around the country with huge success. As one teacher said, "When children are taught how to handle their conflicts, The Win/Win Guidelines alleviate their need to fight." This teacher's words mirror results found by other educators who teach conflict resolution skills. In an extensive study David Johnson and Roger Johnson discovered that "conflict resolution and peer mediation training results in students knowing the negotiation and mediation procedures, being able to use the procedures in actual conflicts, transferring the procedures to nonclassroom conflicts, and transferring the procedures to nonschool conflicts in the home" (*Conflict*, 35).

In the thirteen years since writing the Win/Win Guidelines, I have had countless educators report to me that these guidelines have enabled their students to streamline their communications during a conflict, getting to the core of the problem and resolving it quickly. As one assistant principal said, "The Win/Win Guidelines are posted in every room in the school. Students and staff resolve conflicts with dignity, confidence, and mutual respect. Our students come to school secure in the knowledge that their rights are protected in a humane, systematic, effective manner."

Workshop participants report improvements in resolving their own conflicts as a result of using the Win/Win strategy. As one teacher said, "At first it feels a little strange to communicate in this manner, but over time it becomes second nature." It's like learning to ride a bike: When you first try it, you have to think of every move; and it all feels strange. Even after you have practiced, you still might fall off. But over time you become comfortable and begin to ride with ease. You begin to notice that riding feels as natural as walking, even better. The same may be said for using the Win/Win Guidelines.

Children take to the Win/Win method quickly—the younger the better. Those children who learn in preschool or kindergarten to resolve conflicts by the Win/Win Guidelines soon integrate this method into their lives. As with all peacemaking skills, the later you introduce the guidelines, the more negative socialization you have to undo. Nevertheless, don't become discouraged if you're introducing this strategy to older children. In time, they'll greatly appreciate your efforts, especially as they see their relationships with friends and family improve. As one fifth grader said after learning conflict resolution, "I don't fight as much anymore."

A Word About "I Messages"

By sending I-messages, parents and teachers are also modeling a behavior: they are showing that it is legitimate to tell other persons that you want or need something from them. And they are also modeling that there is a way of communicating their feelings that is not blameful of the other, not threatening, not a put-down. (Gordon, 133)

Throughout this book you can find references to the use of "I messages," a tool for communicating with adults and children alike, both globally and locally. Many family therapists teach "I messages" to couples in counseling to help them communicate without putting their partners on the defensive. Simple declarative statements starting with the word "I," "I messages" help us express our needs and feelings in nonthreatening ways. These statements stand in sharp contrast to "You messages" that can be interpreted as blameful and therefore tend to escalate conflicts.

For example, a friend returns a much-loved book covered with coffee stains. Of course you're angry; who wouldn't be? If you never learned about "I messages," you might find yourself blurting out an automatic response like, "You are so inconsiderate! Look what you did to my book! That's the last time I'll lend you anything!" You both walk away in a huff. Your friend's feelings are wounded, and you're left stewing in your anger. Or perhaps you might stuff your feelings, not say a word to your friend, but call someone else to complain about her or him, and then act aloof the next time you see the person.

Using an "I message" enables you to address the problem assertively but respectfully: "I'm upset that my book has coffee stains all over it. What happened?" In this case, you're giving your friend a chance to respond in a nearly neutral scenario. "I'm so sorry," the friend responds. "My daughter was looking at it when she was home for spring break. She never told me she'd spilled coffee on it. Let me get you another copy." In dealing with the problem directly but nonjudgmentally, you set the groundwork for its ultimate solution. In the first example, you were driven by your automatic response mechanism, jumping to a false conclusion, and placing blame on your friend. By using an attacking "You message," the problem isn't solved, and the friendship is damaged.

"I messages" need to be delivered from a conciliatory place inside of us that values relationships and seeks ways to solve problems. "I messages" are assertive, not aggressive; direct, not abrasive; honest, not attacking. "I messages" help preserve relationships. Adults and children of all ages need to learn how to use them.

Some people recommend avoiding the word "you" completely when delivering an "I message." For example, your spouse is chronically late. You're angry and need to address the problem. Attempting to avoid the word "you," perhaps you would say, "I get upset when people are late. I wish that behavior could come to an end." I find this approach somewhat awkward, even for me, and difficult for children to use. Instead, I recommend including "you" when necessary, but doing so in a tactful way. Tact requires an awareness of one's tone of voice and facial expression. If you include "you" in your statement but do so with sarcasm or a look of vexation, it will come across as attacking. The statement needs to be made with a pure motive: we have a problem to solve, and I'm communicating my concern in hopes of solving it. You might say to your ever-tardy spouse, "I get upset when you're late. It frustrates me because I like to be prompt. What can we do to solve this problem."

Coming from a conciliatory mode is key. We must be more committed to solving the problem than to being right or winning the argument. That's not to say the other person should win the argument instead. It means that both people need to compromise, moving in the direction of each other's needs, working together toward a fair solution. We must be willing to give up our power struggles. "I messages" help us do this. When we teach kids how to use them, we give them a tool for life.

Now lets look inside the classroom to see how "I messages" can be introduced in the context of the Win/Win Guidelines. First you'll see an example for using puppets with primary students, followed by an example for introducing Win/Win to older students.

Introducing Win/Win to Primary Students

Journal Entry: September 12

"Alf and Froggie had a conflict while you were still at home this morning," I told my class as the children sat on the floor before me looking up at the two puppets adorning my hands.

"What happened?" asked Justin.

"Why don't I let them tell you," I responded. I held up Alf first.

"Well, I was just sitting in the book center minding my own business and reading my favorite book, *Frog and Toad*. I put my book down for a minute so I could get a drink, and when I came back to the book center, my book was gone! I looked around, and there sat Froggie at the table reading my book!"

"So what did you do?" I asked.

"I took it away from him, that's what. I grabbed it. I mean, I had it to begin with."

At this point, Froggie chimed in. "Yeah, Alf grabbed it right out of my hands! That wasn't fair!"

"So what did you do?" I asked Froggie.

"I pushed Alf and took my book back," Froggie answered indignantly.

"And then you both started fighting," didn't you, I asked.

Both puppets nodded their heads, and looked down. Alf then looked at the children and said, "And then we had to go to time out."

"You're not supposed to fight in school," ChristiAnne told him.

At this point I turned to my class and said, "Boys and girls, maybe you can help Froggie and Alf solve their conflict. Do you have any suggestions for them?"

About ten hands shot up. I called on Hannah. "Use your words instead of pushing."

"Great idea, Hannah. A little hint I want to give to Alf and Froggie and to all of you is to start from 'I' instead of 'you' when you speak. You can start by saying, "I didn't like it when. . . . That's called an "I message."

Matthew's hand zoomed up, "I know, I know, Alf could have said, 'I didn't like it when you took my book. I was reading it.' He could have done that instead of grabbing. People shouldn't grab. Then they wouldn't have gotten into the fight."

Then I turned to Alf and Froggie and said, "Would you like to try it?"

"Only if he does it too," said Alf.

"OK, I'll do it," said Froggie, somewhat reluctantly

"By the way," I added, "when you tell someone something that's on your mind and you start from 'I' you're giving an I message." I had the children repeat the phrase "I message" after me as I wrote it on the board. "I messages help people work out conflicts." Picking up the puppets again, I resumed the dialogue.

"Alf, could you look into Froggie's eyes and tell him what was on you mind when you saw him holding the book you had just put down. Remember to start with 'I'."

Alf turned to Froggie and said, "Froggie, I got really angry when I saw you with my book. I was right in the middle of reading it, and I just got up to get a drink of water and then you took it. That wasn't fair."

"Alf," I said, "that was a great 'I message.' You expressed exactly what you felt and you didn't use any put-downs. Now, Froggie I'm going to ask you to look at Alf and say back in your own words what you just heard him say to you. Start with 'I heard you say' and then just repeat back in you own words what he said."

Froggie turned to Alf and said, "I heard you say that you were angry because you got up to get a drink and when you came back I was reading

your book. You said that wasn't fair. But I didn't even know you were reading it!"

I turned to Alf and said, "Did he understand what was bothering you?" Alf nodded yes.

I now looked at Froggie and said, "Would you look into Alf's eyes and give him an 'I message' expressing what was on **your** mind."

Froggie looked at Alf and said, "I was looking for something to read, so I walked over to the book center. There on the floor was a book with a frog on the cover, just like me! Well, I got so excited I picked it up and brought it over to the table so I could read it right away. I didn't know you had it first!"

"Good 'I message,' Froggie." Now, Alf would you look into Froggie's eyes and say back what you heard **him** say. Remember to start with 'I heard you say.'

Alf looked at Froggie and said, "I heard you say that you didn't know I was even reading *Frog and Toad*. You got so excited about seeing the frog on the cover that you just picked up the book and started reading it?"

"Right," said Froggie. "I didn't mean to start anything." Here I added, "What other choice could Alf have made, instead of grabbing?"

The children were on their knees now, waving their hands. "I know!" said Terrence, "Alf could have given an 'I message' instead of grabbing. That's what I'm gonna do next time someone has something I want."

"What an excellent idea, Terrence," I chimed in happily. "Boys and girls, I think Terrence has a terrific idea for all of us."

"Froggie could have said an 'I message' instead of pushing," added Caitlin.

"Wow, boys and girls," I exclaimed. "You're all so good at this! I wish you had been here early this morning. You could have prevented this conflict from happening."

"Hey, that's on our chart," said Matthew, gesturing toward our Guidelines for a Peaceful Classroom.

Other voices started chiming in. Almost immediately, Kristina pointed to the abbreviated Win/Win Guidelines on our peacemaking bulletin board, saying, "Isn't this what we just did?"

"That's right, Kristina, we all just helped Alf and Froggie resolve their conflict using the Win/Win Guidelines, and guess what: That's exactly what you can do next time you have a conflict. Instead of fighting, you can talk it out the same way you just helped Froggie and Alf do it. What do you think?"

Scott answered, smiling, "My mom sure would be happy if I did this with my big brother."

I encouraged the children to try using the Win/Win Guidelines on their own instead of coming to me next time a conflict arises, adding, "If you can't remember the whole process, just remember to give the other person an 'I message' and then try to find a solution together."

I don't expect the children to remember every step, but I hope they've picked up something about the spirit of this process. That's what I'm looking for, an inner shift that makes them see that rather than fighting, arguing or withdrawing they can use a strategy that helps them move beyond hurt feelings and into a mode of shared problem solving.

Introducing Win/Win to Grades 3-6

One of the most effective ways to introduce conflict resolution to intermediate and upper grade students is by staging a conflict with another teacher in front of the class. An example follows.

(Mrs. Jones is about to teach a math lesson. Unbeknownst to her class she has asked Mr. Kim to come in at this moment and pick an argument with her.)

Mrs. Jones: Ok, boys and girls, take out your math books.

Mr. Kim (walking in irately): Mrs. Jones, you have inconvenienced me to no end! You still have the math guide I lent you a week ago. I must have asked you three times in the past week to give it back, and I need it *right now!*"

Mrs. Jones: (defensive): Can't you see I'm about to teach a math lesson. I can't give it back now. I need it to refer to for my lesson.

Mr. Kim (annoyed): Use your own guide!

Mrs. Jones: (raising her voice): I can't! Don't you remember? Mine was ruined when the roof was leaking after that big storm last week.

Mr. Kim (raising his voice): That's not my problem!

Mrs. Jones (angrily): Get out of my room! You can't just barge in here and interrupt my class! Besides, I have to teach this math lesson!

Mr. Kim (shouting): How am *I* supposed to teach math? You've had my guide for a week!

Mrs. Jones (shouting): If you don't get out of my room right now, I'm going to call Mr. Blaine (the principal). Do you understand?!

Mr. Kim: The only thing I understand is that I'm not leaving this room without my guide!

The kids are stark silent, eyes riveted to the front of the room, never having witnessed this kind of scene in school before. Both teachers stop arguing and turn to the class.

Mrs. Jones: Boys and girls, Mr. Kim and I really aren't mad at each other. We staged this conflict to get your attention. We believe that conflicts and put-downs are big problems among kids. We want to help you look for better ways to solve problems.

"How did you feel when you saw Mr. Kim and me yelling at each other?"

Megan: Scared! I didn't think teachers acted that way.

John: Embarrassed. You're supposed to be professionals.

Larry: Cool. It reminded me of something on TV, but it really was a little weird too. I guess I really didn't like hearing you talk to each other that way.

Tamika: I couldn't believe you were yelling at each other like that! I thought you guys were good friends. I'm so relieved it was only pretend. (A lot of kids nodded.)

Mr. Kim: Mrs. Jones and I *are* good friends. That's why we decided to do this together. We want the kids in our school to start rethinking the way they handle conflict. Did we sound like people you know?

Larry: Yeah, my parents. (Everybody laughed, some of them nervously.)

Mrs. Jones: We've certainly heard a lot of kids acting the way we did, so we figured you would relate. Would you help us come up with solutions to this conflict as though it were real? We're hoping you can think of better ways that we could have handled it.

Larry: That's cool. You mean we don't have to do math right now?

Mrs. Jones: Not right now. We're going to take the time to do some conflict resolution first. Give us some suggestions as to how we could have handled our problem.

Megan: Well, first of all, Mr. Kim didn't have to come barging into our room like that. He could have talked to you privately.

Mrs. Jones: And what could he have said? Carlos: He could have said, "I really need my guide back today. You've had it all week."

Mr. Kim: So I should have started with the word "I," Is that right?

Carlos: Yeah, it sounds nicer.

Mr.Kim: Carlos, what you've just described is called an "I message." That's the best kind of statement to make, one that starts with "I," when you have a problem. It doesn't put the other person on the defensive. Did you notice how defensive Mrs. Jones became when I spoke to her in an attacking way, saying, "You're so inconsiderate"?

Diedre: Yeah, but she should have given back your book when you asked her for it. I don't blame you for getting angry.

John: But he didn't have to sound so mean.

Mr. Kim: What else could I have said?

Megan: You could have said, "I've asked you to return my guide a number of times. I really need it now."

Tamika: And you could have said it without sounding so angry.

Mr. Kim: That's true. Maybe I needed to cool off a little before I approached her.

Tom: You mean like get a drink of water or something. That's what I do.

Mr. Kim: That's right, Tom. Things like getting a drink of water, counting to ten, taking a deep breath—any of those things can help you cool off when you're angry. Then you can talk to the other person with a clearer head.

Diedre: But what about you, Mrs. Jones? You shouldn't have kept Mr. Kim's guide for so long. You talked mean to Mr. Kim too. You even tried to throw him out of our room, and then you were gonna tattle on him to Mr. Blaine! (The kids laughed.)

Mrs. Jones: You're right, Diedre. I, too, needed to take responsibility for what I had done. Maybe if I had said, "Gee, Mr. Kim, I'm really sorry I kept your guide so long," he might not have acted so angry.

Mr. Kim: What do you think we could have done to work out the problem?

John: You could have cooled off first, then you could have told Mrs. Jones you really needed your book back.

Theodore: Or you could have left a note in her mailbox saying you needed the book today.

Diedre: Or Mrs. Jones could have returned the guide right away instead of keeping it for a week. She could have made copies of the pages she needed.

Larry: Or she could have gone to Mr. Blain and asked him if he had another guide for her to use.

Tanya: Or she could have borrowed someone else's guide.

Megan: Or she could have asked Mr. Kim to share his guide with her.

Larry: Or maybe she could have stopped teaching math! (The class cracked up.)

Mrs. Jones: Boys and girls, you have come up with many solutions to this problem. And, know what? Most problems have a variety of solutions. You just have to be willing to look for them.

Mr. Kim (hanging up the Win/Win Guidelines): Mrs. Jones and I want to share something with you that can help with conflicts. These six simple steps are the Win/Win Guidelines that will help you work out just about any conflict you might have, even with your parents. (The class laughed again.)

Mrs. Jones: In fact you talked about a number of these steps yourselves, like giving "I messages, cooling off, taking responsibility, and brainstorming solutions.

Mr. Kim: Let's look at the steps together. Then you can help Mrs. Jones and me decide on the solution to our problem that's likely to settle it once and for all.

Reflections

Today's lessons had a dual purpose: They provided a strategy for the children to negotiate conflicts, and they increased their thinking skills. By providing their own endings for each conflict situation, the children were, in essence, bringing the plot to a close. In doing so, they engaged in the processes of problem solving and perceiving outcomes, skills paramount to both conflict resolution and writing.

In William Kreidler's book, *Creative Conflict Resolution*, he said, "All conflict resolution involves communication. That is not to suggest that communication in and of itself is a panacea. When it comes to conflict, we do not need more communication, we need better communication" (83). I couldn't agree more. By providing the children with a strategy for resolving conflicts, we

give them a way to work out the problems that inevitably come up in school and in life. Hurt feelings, disagreements, unintended insults, disputes over materials, and differing perceptions are all inherent in human interaction. When we can help children interact more skillfully with one another, we give them a gift they can take with them on any avenue they walk along through life.

When Peaceful Methods Are Challenged

An interesting thing happened after I introduced the Win/Win Guidelines. Terrence, intently pondering the scenario we had just talked about, said, "I know you want us to use our words to work out conflicts, but my mom told me that if anyone hits me I should hit them back." This, unfortunately is not an uncommon reaction from parents.

"Terrence," I said, "Your mom wants you to be safe, and that's why she's telling you to hit. She doesn't want anyone to hurt you. But remember the story of the Peaceful Warrior where Danny stood up to the bully by being strong and respectful. He used his words, not his hands, to work our the conflict; and he ended up with a friend, not an enemy. Do you remember that?"

"Yes," said Terrence. "But my mom said I should hit back."

"Terrence, the way we keep children safe in this school is to teach them the Win/Win Guidelines and to help them learn to work out their problems so they don't have to fight. You're being braver and safer by using your words. But you have to stand tall like this," I had him lift his carriage to its fullest height and hold his head up high.

"Then you need to look the person in the eye and say, 'This isn't worth fighting about. Let's talk it out.'" We practiced saying the words together, standing tall and brave, just like Danny did in the story.

"But what if they still want to hit me?" he asked, considering what I had said, but still skeptical.

"Then you keep standing tall, look them in the eye, and say, 'This isn't worth getting in trouble over. I want to work out this problem with you.'" Then walk away with your head held high, your body strong, and ask an adult or peer mediator to help the two of you work out the problem."

"Isn't that tattling, if I go to a grown-up?" Terrence asked, mulling it over.

"No," I replied, "only if you go to an adult with the intention of getting the other person in trouble. If you really care about working out the problem, you won't be tattling."

"Are you sure?" asked Terrence.

"I'm sure," I said. "Just make sure your motives are pure."

"OK," said Terrence, smiling, "I'll try it."

"That's wonderful, Terrence," I said. "It's very brave of you to consider this, and I know it will be scary the first time you try it; but it's braver to do it this way than to fight."

"Just like Martin Luther King," added Terrence.

"That's right," I said, smiling inside.

At conference time I repeated this conversation with Terrence's mother, reassuring her that we both had the same goals: the safety and well-being of her child. I asked her to give the peacemaking program a chance when Terrence is in school, and to trust that the system we are using will ultimately keep him safer than will fighting. We discussed her fears that Terrence was small for his age and that he might be picked on by other kids. I described to her how I'd shown Terrence to stand tall and walk strong and never to feel less powerful because of his height, reminding him that true power comes from the inside. I also reassured Terrence's mom that indeed we were creating a peaceful school in which all of the children were expected to abide by the same standards: respect for others, and no fighting. Although my words flew in the face of all that she had grown up with, she trusted me and she trusted our school, aware of an overall feeling of respect and cooperation that had been fostered through our peacemaking program. With reservation, she agreed to give it a try.

Terry Salinger, Director of Research for the International Reading Association, used to come into my room to chat, observe, and see how teaching peacemaking had an impact on the students' literacy development. We talked about peacemaking as a tool for building the kind of trust and comfort children need to feel confident writing, learning, and taking risks. In her book, *Literacy for Young Children*, Salinger urged teachers, citing my classroom as an example, to "talk openly about issues of values, trust and respect" (96). The conversation with Terrence and his mother typifies many talkes between teacher and parents in the ongoing effort to build trust and respect and provide lasting peacemaking strategies to children and their parents.

Both Terrence and his mother were encouraged to see things from another point of view. Perceiving another's viewpoint is key in using the Win/Win Guidelines. The children must learn how to reflect upon the feelings of another person in order to resolve conflicts. Fran Schmidt in her book (with Friedman), *Creative Conflict Solving For Kids*, said, "Conflict is a natural part of our lives. Conflicts arise over misunderstandings, unmet needs, different values and perceptions. Children can be taught to deal constructively with conflicts. When channeled into positive action, conflict stimulates creativity and problem-solving ability" (iii). Teaching conflict resolution skills helps children not only with conflict, but with problem-solving and creativity, thus helping in all areas of the curriculum, including oral expression and writing. The same strategy we employ in envisioning a peaceful classroom or the solution to a problem can be used in envisioning a story to write. In fact, one process reinforces the other.

Postscript

With continual reinforcement, Terrence was able to stay out of fights; and his mother came to see that children can keep themselves safe by working out conflicts rather than fighting. The daily infusion of peacemaking concepts into our school helped alter the thinking of Terrence and other children like him.

Is this approach foolproof? No. There are no absolute solutions to any problem, and no magical approaches that work under all circumstances. But there are subtle and sometimes major changes that can occur when we teach from our deepest convictions.

In schools committed to peacemaking I have seen teachers who learn to live and model the peacemaking skills they teach, integrating them into daily discussions, reinforcing their students' positive behaviors, and finding creative ways to uphold the philosophy day after day. Before long, children begin thinking and acting differently, softening in their attitudes, listening to one another more attentively, displaying greater compassion, and resolving conflicts rather than quarreling. Do conflicts disappear? Absolutely not, but the way children respond to conflict changes profoundly. Moreover, children begin to think about their attitudes, actions, and choices. Little by little change takes root. As I saw with both Terrence and his mother, trusting the process takes time. As Sara Ban Breathnach wrote, "Lasting change happens in infinitesimal increments: a day, an hour, a minute, a heartbeat at a time" (page 1/11). The change I am speaking of is fundamental and does not happen all at once. Does change happen with every child? I believe some form of change will occur in most children if we teach peacemaking from the heart and weave it into the fabric of everything we do. For children who have been deeply wounded, change may be very slow and largely internal. But sometimes, the most difficult children are also the most responsive to peacemaking, as in the case of Teddy, a child you will meet in Chapter 4.

Of utmost importance is your own faith in the process of peacemaking. Several years ago I surveyed a group of fifth grade children who had been learning peacemaking since kindergarten. When the children were asked what was the most important influence in making the program successful, the majority answered, "My teachers' belief in peacemaking and the examples they set."

Teaching, it has been said, is an act of faith. So it is with the teaching of peacemaking. We must continuously find ways to bolster our faith in the process, through partnership with colleagues, related readings, daily personal practices such as prayer or meditation—anything that keeps us in touch with our highest purpose as educators and as human beings. We must keep a healthy sense of idealism. As Helen Keller observed, "No pessimist ever discovered the secrets of the stars, or sailed to an uncharted land, or opened a new heaven to the human spirit" (qtd. in *Random Acts of Kindness*, 1998).

Envision yourself as a sailor into uncharted waters, defining a course that will affect the thoughts and actions of your students—for the rest of their lives. Your role is *that* important.

Building a Climate of Respect

> . . . *a workable planetary culture, to which almost every human being could subscribe, is a culture of civility.* (M. Scott Peck, 346)

Four elements are vital in building an atmosphere of respect: fostering good listening, providing affirmation, expecting success, and setting ethical standards. Each essential element is discussed in the following paragraphs.

Fostering Good Listening Skills

"Giving another person the gift of your listening is the highest form of respect," I tell the children every year. Listening is a skill that can be devel-

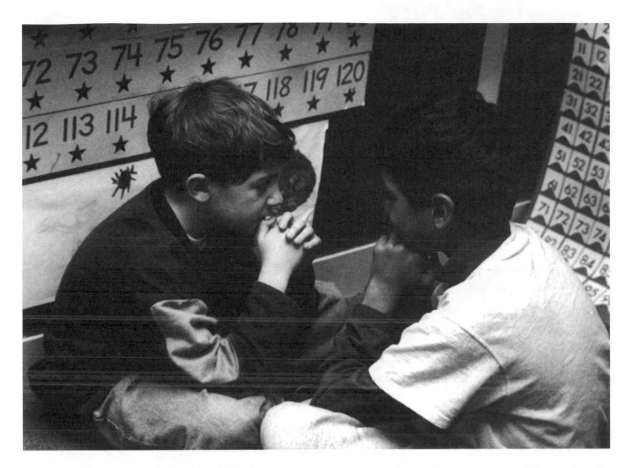

oped, and when we teach this skill early we provide children with something invaluable.

Think about the good feeling that comes from being listened to. When someone listens with his or her heart, we feel validated, cared for, and respected. And we want to be around that person more. The same holds true for children. Their relationships thrive and grow as a result of good listening.

"Please look at me," said Kristin before she started to speak. She looked at the faces of her classmates before beginning. When all eyes were on her, bodies still, and voices silent, she began to speak. This practice is one I teach my class on the first day of school. It's a practice that continues throughout the year, one which I am diligent about, knowing that my students learn better when they listen well. Also, my life as a teacher is easier when my students are good listeners.

Build this skill first by modeling it. Listen without interrupting a child, suspend your own thoughts and try to empathize with what is being said. Be aware of your nonverbal language when you listen, leaning toward the speaker, avoiding looking around, and nodding occasionally. Ask the children to do the same, and during class discussions caution them *never* to begin speaking until everyone clearly demonstrates listening.

The Quiet Sign (two fingers up like the peace sign) is an effective way to get children to focus. I always say, "When you see me hold up the Quiet Sign, stop whatever you're doing, even if you're in the middle of a sentence, hold up the Quiet Sign yourself, and look directly at me."

We practice doing this very quickly, making it into a game initially. "When I hold up the Quiet Sign see if you can become quiet this fast," I tell them, snapping my fingers. Then I'll tell the class to start talking. In a few moments, I'll say, "Quiet Sign," and hold up the fingers of my left hand in the sign while snapping the fingers of my right hand. The children enjoy seeing how quickly they can quiet themselves and hold up the Quiet Sign along with me. Before long, I can give the "Quiet Sign" with the accompanying words, and the children become quiet in an instant.

Whenever a child in the class wants to speak they ask for the class's attention as Kristen did above. The speaker looks around before speaking to make sure everyone is looking and ready to listen. If someone is not, the speaker then requests their attention again. How empowering it is for children to know they can command the respect of their classmates, and that what they have to say is important. Research has shown that all group processes flourish when people listen to each other actively and with empathy. In contrast, when listening skills are poor, problems develop.

The Process of Affirmation

One of the methods used to build self-esteem and reinforce respectful behaviors is the process of affirmation—the giving of sincere, appropriate praise. When we see what's good in our students and affirm them for those qualities, we hold up a mirror showing them what is positive in themselves. The more teachers can hold up a positive mirror to children, the more we help their self-esteem to grow. They can then look out through the window of their evolving selves and more clearly see the positive qualities of others.

By modeling affirmation, we also encourage children to affirm each other. "Max, you did so well on your spelling test today," says Gianna, with a big smile. "Thank you, Gianna, so did you," says Max. smiling back. Through communications like this, care and encouragement flow. Acceptance and respect are reinforced, thus nurturing the atmosphere of peace in the classroom.

Teachers need to be cognizant of how we affirm, though, making sure that our affirmations are sincere and appropriate. In Michele Borba's book, *Esteem Builders*, she stated that for praise

to be effective it must be

• Deserved
• Immediate
• Behavior-centered
• Individual
• Specific
• Repeated
• Spontaneous (52)

"Alyssia, I noticed how caring you were toward Sam just now. You noticed that she was having trouble with her math paper, and you offered to help her without being asked. It makes me feel good as your teacher to see that kind of considerateness, and it sets a good example for others. Thanks for being that way." This kind of affirmation is far more powerful than a generalization like, "Alyssia, you're such a nice girl." By specifying exactly what Alyssia had done, I not only affirmed her, but reinforced the positive behavior as well. What we give attention to continues. By affirming positive actions and catching children in the act of doing things right, we enable good behavior to continue, negative behavior to stop.

Throughout the first day of school, and on all subsequent days, affirm your students as often as possible; also, praise the whole class at times, letting them know how proud you are of their growing listening skills, respectful actions, and good choices. A simple "thanks for listening" is worth a thousand reprimands.

The Gift of High Expectations

Trust, respect, support, and high expectations must be generously and genuinely present for all children. (Routman, 29)

When children walk into my classroom on the first day of school, I expect them all to behave properly, regardless of histories, family difficulties, classifications, or labels. I continuously expect all of the children to treat each other with respect, interacting as peacemakers all year long. True, each child isn't necessarily equipped with the skills to do so right away. Nevertheless, I hold this vision for every child that I teach, and I have never been disappointed. Yes, good behavior is a challenge for some children; but I've consistently seen children move in the direction of the vision I hold for them, despite their challenges. The same thinking relates to academics. Teachers increase the likelihood of learning simply by expecting it to happen—and supporting the learners in the process.

Harvard psychologist Robert Rosenthal studied the effect of teacher expectations on children's learning. He discovered that ". . . children whose teachers had confidence in their ability to learn showed IQ gains of fifteen to to twenty-seven points" (qtd. in Briggs, *Your Child's Self-Esteem*, 49). So it is with children's ability to be peacemakers. If we believe they can, they will. We help children succeed when we expect the best from them; and in doing so, we enable them to fulfill their promise academically, socially, and ethically.

National speaker Carl Boyd (keynote speaker at South Brunswick District In-Service Day, 1995) told the story of a teacher assigned to a class of low achievers one year. No one told the teacher about the children's ability, however. When the teacher received the class list, she noticed that it contained each child's first and last name, followed by a three-digit number that she assumed to be their I.Q.s. The teacher was delighted to see the high number next to each child's name and surmised that she had been given an exceptionally bright class. Consequently, her expectations were very high; and she piled on challenging work. By the end of the year, the entire class excelled as their teacher had expected. What a shock when that teacher discovered that the three-digit numbers were not I.Q.s—but locker numbers! Expectations of success are critical.

Setting Ethical Standards

. . . character is how you behave when no one is looking. (Robert Coles, Moral, 198)

Ethical standards are the soil for growth of positive attitudes, choices, and behaviors. Standards are not rules, but concepts by which to live. By defining clear, consistent, non-negotiable standards for all children, we set the ethical foundation for peacemaking. Again, modeling is key.

Chapter 1 includes an example of a class discussion from which guidelines were developed. The ethical standards held by the teacher for he class should be integrated into such a discussion. Often with minimal prompting, or none at all, the children will begin talking about the same standards that are important to you. Here are the ethical standards I hold for my students.

- We treat each other with respect at all times.
- We don't hurt each other physically, verbally, or emotionally.
- We respect the rights and property of others.
- We tell the truth.
- We accept differences.

As mentioned before, these standards are non-negotiable; there is never an excuse for breaking them. Each teacher needs to decide how he or she will handle noncompliance with standards. In my school we have specific consequences for fighting and speaking racial slurs. For the other standards, the consequences are up to the discretion of individual teachers. The essential point is this: Failure to comply with standards must never be ignored. The problem should be addressed immediately, letting the child know that what he or she has done is unacceptable.

Standards are critical to building what psychiatrist Robert Coles referred to as "moral intelligence." In his book, *The Moral Intelligence of Children*, Coles explained the concept of moral intelligence.

We grow morally as a consequence of learning how to be with others, how to behave in this world, a learning prompted by taking to heart what we have seen and heard. The child is witness; the child is an ever-attentive witness of grown-up morality—or lack thereof; the child looks and looks for cues as to how one ought to behave, and finds them galore as we parents and teachers go about our lives, making choices, addressing people, showing in action our rock-bottom assumptions, desires, values, and thereby telling those young observers much more than we may realize. (5)

What we choose to emphasize and model are crucial. In an optimal situation, standards are honored schoolwide and supported by every member of the educational community. Some teachers express frustration because they tried hard to reinforce proper behavior and respect in their classes, but their efforts were thwarted by a lack of common purpose among teachers and administrators in the same school building. In cases like this, teachers feel that their efforts are thwarted once their children leave the room. Talk to your principals about creating schoolwide standards and implementing peacemaking throughout your building. You'll improve the quality of life in your school by doing so.

CHAPTER Three

The First Month of School

Children learn openness, sharing, positive self-concepts and cooperation,
not by being told about them, but by becoming part of a community in which
these attributes are the norm.

—Priscilla Prutzman, (5)

In this chapter we'll take a look at ways to integrate and reinforce peacemaking, creating a bridge between the first weeks of school and the ensuing year. The more deliberate teachers are in our efforts to model and integrate the skills of peacemaking, the more apt we will be to create a sturdy bridge for our students to walk across all year long.

Some questions to consider at this point include the following.

- Am I taking care of myself? Am I applying what I have learned to feel peaceful, calm, and relatively centered in my own life?
- Am I modeling the skills of peacemaking? Do I teach by example, sharing my own successes, struggles, and growth in this area, thus enabling the children to learn from my experiences?
- Do I have clear consistent standards that I expect all of my students to abide by; e.g., we

don't fight; put-downs of any kind are unacceptable; we listen while others speak?
- Have I integrated conflict resolution enough for the children to see it as a natural part of the way people interact?
- Am I affirming the children often, catching them in the act of positive behaviors and acknowledging them?
- Do I have a child-centered classroom that reflects the passions and interests of the individual children in it?
- Does my room exemplify peacemaking? Is it bright, inviting, and adorned with peacemaking-related bulletin boards, posters, poems, and children's work?
- Do I empower my students to make responsible choices?
- Am I keeping parents informed about peacemaking activities and educating them in the process?

- Am I integrating peacemaking into my daily activities through writing, literature, classroom discussions, and other curriculum areas?
- I appreciating small steps, resisting the expectation that a peaceful classroom will happen overnight?

Remember to have patience, faith, and to rejoice in the results you see, no matter how small. Teaching peacemaking is like teaching any other skill; it doesn't come all at once. Much of your work will be in changing old habits, old thinking patterns, and old ways of looking at life. All of this takes hard work, perseverance, and a belief that change is possible. Congratulate yourself for small steps along the way.

Now let's go back to the classroom and take another look inside.

Fostering Collaboration

Journal Entry: September 21

Today we picked a year-long class goal: to be good peacemakers. First we brainstormed, then the children voted and unanimously chose this goal over all others. I'm realizing how much children tend to value what the teacher prizes. Right now the class is working on a large mural to illustrate their visions of a peaceful classroom, all twenty-two of them sprawled on the floor in two long lines, each child designing, drawing, coloring, talking. I'm curious to see if they'll be able to put their early lessons in peacemaking into practice and negotiate the sharing of markers, crayons, and pencils without any direct intervention from me. After putting on a listening tape called "Work the Anger Out," I've assumed the role of observer, deliberately stepping aside so the children can work independently. I'm also curious to see what will happen and wondering if this mural will be a patchwork of each child's ideas or a cohesive vision of a peaceful classroom.

It seems that all the wiggling bodies working at the same time have caused a large hill of paper to rise between Tommy and Prem. I'm wondering if they'll see this as a problem they can solve together or a reason for conflict. Tommy first tried to flatten the bump with his hand. When that didn't work, he stopped and thought for a minute, then turned to Prem, gesturing toward the hill between them and said, "Pass the bump down." He and Prem raised their bodies, smoothed the paper they had been working on, and pushed the hill to the next person.

"Mary Lynn, pass the bump," Prem chimed in. One by one, hands were lifted and paper flattened as the bump moved from child to child. I watched and smiled as the 20-foot mural began to flatten, having done nothing myself to make it happen.

I noticed Erica grab the red marker Chris had just put down. Chris, flushing, opened his mouth to say something, closed it as though catching himself, took a breath and turned to Erica. He said irately, "I don't like it when you take my markers." Erica didn't respond. She continued coloring, pretending she didn't hear Chris.

"Hey, Erica, I'm talking to you," Chris said, a little more annoyed.

"What did you say?" asked Erica, looking at him this time. Chris repeated his initial statement.

"Oh," said Erica, putting the marker down.

"Hey, you're supposed to repeat what I say," admonished Chris.

Erica turned to him this time and said, "I heard you say you didn't like when I took the markers."

"That's right," said Chris, "It annoys me."

"OK, I'm sorry," Erica reluctantly replied. Can you share the red marker with me? I needed it to color the girl's dress."

"All you had to do was ask," said Chris. He agreed to let her use the marker until he needed it, and both children continued drawing.

The class began to sing along with the tape as each child negotiated the use of materials and space. Finally complete, their finished product held together and actually looked like a mural. Through informal talking and sharing, the children found ways to connect their ideas and work together as a team.

Reflections

Stepping back and giving the children the opportunity to put peacemaking skills into practice is important for both teachers and students. As teachers, we too often step in and supervise everything. Given full ownership of the day's activity, the children not only produced a unique product; but they also successfully tested the waters of collaboration and negotiation, and realized they could work out the problems that arose among them.

Peacemaking means building self-discipline within each child. When teachers guide children to interact with others responsibly, working out conflicts along the way, we help them build a greater sense of mastery. The resolution of problems and formulation of decisions between peers needs to rest ultimately with the children. Teachers often must move out of the way for it to happen.

Our most direct guidance in problem solving and conflict resolution needs to be given early in the year. As time goes on, a teacher will be able to step back more and more. Within a few months, a growing sense of independence begins to surface; and children can be encouraged to resolve conflicts by themselves in a quiet part of the room. "Get back to me and let me know what solution you've decided upon," is all a teacher may need to say, intervening only if the children are unable to self-mediate. In most cases our intervention will not be necessary because the children will have internalized the skills needed to work out their own problems. We saw the beginnings of this today.

Showcasing Conflict Resolution

Showcasing conflict resolution is done by mediating a dispute in front of the entire class with the permission of the disputants. In doing this demonstration, a teacher enables a whole class to become familiar with the conflict resolution process and gives children opportunities to offer solutions. Everybody gains: the disputants from hearing the input of the class, and the class from the practice in conflict resolution strategies. An added bonus: Through this process children learn that everyone has conflicts, many of them similar, and that conflicts have solutions.

Journal Entry: September 20

There was conflict today between Chris and Prem over "cutting" when it was time to line up. This was a perfect opportunity to reinforce how a conflict is mediated using the Win/Win Guidelines.

"Mrs. Drew, Prem cut me in line," Chris complained to me, with a look if annoyance. "I was here first."

"Chris, did you speak to Prem directly before coming to me?"

"No," replied Chris looking down at the floor.

I said, "Go get Prem (who had gone to the water fountain) and I'll help you work this out together." The rest of the class was in line, and we had a few minutes before lunch. I asked the boys if it would be okay with them to discuss their problem in front of the class, and they both agreed to do so.

"Chris," I said "would you look at Prem and tell him what's on your mind. Don't forget to start with 'I.'" (This was my prompt for getting Chris to use an "I Message.") I had the two boys face each other, and I stayed at their sides as they began to speak.

"Prem, I didn't like it when you cut me in line. I was there first."

I turned to Prem next. "Prem, could you say back to Chris in your own words what you just heard him say? Start with the words, 'I heard you say.' "

"I heard you say that you didn't like it when I cut you in line; but I didn't cut you; you were over there," Prem said, gesturing toward the lunchbox area.

I turned to Chris. "Chris, could you say back what you just heard Prem say."

"I heard you say that you didn't cut me,'cause I was over there," Chris pointed to the lunchboxes. "Well, I just got out of line for a minute to get my lunchbox; and you came up and took my place—but I was there first."

"What can you both do to work out this problem?" I asked.

Prem looked up at me and said, "I think Chris should go to the end of the line because he got out of line to get his lunchbox."

"Prem, look directly at Chris when you speak because the two of you need to work this out. I'm not going to solve it for you."

At this point a few of the other children raised their hands. (When we showcase conflict resolution, it's helpful to allow other class members to contribute solutions, as long as there's no judgment or blaming.) I called on Dominic. "Maybe they both can go to the end. Chris shouldn't be able to get back in line if he left to get his lunchbox, and Prem shouldn't have run up to take his place."

"Prem, didn't you know I just got out of my place for a minute?" Chris inquired. I saw you rushing over to be first as soon as I moved out of line.".

"Is that true, Prem?" I added.

Prem looked down at the floor. "Don't worry. You won't get in trouble if you just tell the truth. Your honesty is very important to me," I told Prem as he looked up. I looked softly into his eyes, hoping to convey the fact that he could trust what I was saying.

Holding my gaze he said, "Yes, it's true. I wanted to be first."

Directing the boys to look at each other again, I said, "How were you each responsible for the problem?"

Chris said, "I guess I shouldn't have tried to get back in line after leaving my place."

Prem replied, I shouldn't have run over to take Chris's place. I know we're not supposed to run."

"Guys, I'm proud of you for taking responsibility in such an honest way," I said.

"How do you think you can solve this problem?"

Chris replied, "I guess we should both go to the end; what do you think, Prem?"

Prem looked at Chris, smiled, and said, "OK, that sounds fair."

Another child said, "Mrs. Drew, why don't we put together a line leader chart, and that way everyone will get a turn."

"Great idea," I said, and then turned to the boys again. "Is there anything the two of you want to say or do right now to show that you feel okay about each other and how you worked out your conflict?"

Chris held out his hand to shake Prem's, smiled,and said, "Thanks for working it out, buddy."

Prem, shook Chris's hand and responded, "Yeah, thanks." They walked to the end of the line together. I profusely acknowledged both of them for their willingness to work out their conflict in an honest and respectful way. (The whole process took less than five minutes.)

I next turned to the class. "Isn't this a better way to work out your problems than fighting, name-calling, or tattling?"

They nodded their heads quietly. For those who weren't taught peacemaking before, this idea was completely new. I will continue to seize as many opportunities as I can to reinforce the Win/Win method, each time enabling the children to see the value of talking out their problems as opposed to fighting. Thanks, Chris and Prem, for the opportunity.

Reflections

Conflicts like this one come up often in the course of a day and can sap the time of teachers and students alike. Being able to negotiate one's way out of conflict is essential to the smooth running of a class. Many teachers have shared with me their frustration at losing valuable chunks of class time on petty conflicts. A third grade teacher said, "I feel so burdened. It seems like I spend half my day listening to kids complain about each other. I'm looking for a way to help kids manage their own behavior, so I don't have to constantly do it for them!" Many teachers feel this way. When they bring peacemaking skills into their classrooms, they notice things starting to change.

Showcasing is one of the most effective tools for reinforcing conflict resolution strategies. When children observe conflicts being worked out, they start to integrate the strategy into their own behavior. Taking time to showcase early and often at the start of the year will help prevent disputes. A conciliatory mode starts to develop in the class as children become more confident in their collective ability to handle problems. They feel empowered by their ability to work out conflicts rather than depending on an adult to do it for them.

The time you invest showcasing at the beginning of the year will come back to you doubled as your children internalize the lessons of peace. Ultimately you will find yourself with more time to teach.

How and When to Mediate

Obviously you're not going to mediate every conflict that occurs. My rule of thumb is that I always try to get the children to mediate on their own first. At the beginning of the year, though, they'll need more assistance in doing this—as in the previous scenario—than they will later. By mid- to late-October children should be somewhat comfortable with the process, and you should be able to send them off to a "Work It Out" spot to self-mediate. Always ask the disputants to get back to you and tell you the solution they came up with.

Many schools have the following abbreviated Win/Win Guidelines printed on "business cards" to give to each child.

Abbreviated Win/Win Guidelines

1. Cool off.
2. "I message."
3. Say back.
4. Take responsibility.
5. Brainstorm solutions.
6. Affirm, forgive, or thank.

Children can pull out their cards and use them as guides when they have conflicts. The more you role play and showcase resolutions of conflicts early in the year, the more adept children will become at resolving their conflicts independently as time goes on.

If a conflict is recurrent or serious, I generally will mediate it. Another situation I'll often mediate is one involving triangles which can be too complex for children to handle on their own. As noted before, my school has peer mediators to help with conflicts. In schools that have conflict resolution programs with no peer mediation, children who have a natural knack for peacemaking will often step in and help their peers. Early in the year, however, you will want to select some common conflicts like the one you just read about to mediate in front of the class for the purpose of showcasing. The showcasing gives children valuable practice in the art of conflict resolution.

There are a number of things you will need to remember when you mediate a conflict.

- *Make sure the children have cooled off enough.* If either party is still too angry to sincerely work out the problem, try mediating later, or the following day.
- *Have the children face each other and speak to each other directly.* You should stand off to the side. Let them own the process.
- *Make sure the children speak to each other respectfully*—no negative faces, body language, or tone of voice. Sarcasm is absolutely unacceptable.
- *Don't allow the children to interrupt each other.* Remind them the first time one tries to interrupt the other. If the interruptions continue, stop the process.
- *Don't take sides.* Allow the children to discuss the problem with each other as thoroughly as they need to after giving their "I messages." Make sure each child reflects ("says back") what the other has said. You can help the process by reflecting what you hear from time to time, summarizing the main points. A teacher's summary is especially helpful if the mediation get stuck.
- *Allow the children to come up with their own solutions.* Don't do it for them. The only way for children to take full ownership of the mediation process is to recognize their ability to self-mediate.

With kindergartners and preschoolers you will want to abbreviate the process. Start by making sure the children are cooled off (essential at any age). Have them sit or stand facing each other and say to one child, "Tell (*the other child*) what's on your mind, starting from 'I.'" Then encourage the other person to reflect, "Tell (*the first child*) what you heard, starting with 'I heard you say. . . .'" Have each child do this. Then ask, "How do you want to solve your problem?" Let them come up with their own solutions, but give prompts if necessary. Lastly, have the childrn shake hands, hug, or thank each other.

Difficult Children/Difficult Situations

The longer I teach the more I see children coming to school with a variety of problems. The children with the biggest problems are the ones who benefit most from peacemaking. Teachers in workshops, despairing over their most difficult students, often say, "Peacemaking sounds great, but it will never work with Pat." My reply usually is, "If you are willing to put in the extra time, effort, and love to reach that child, you probably will." Most elementary-aged children are still reachable. If teachers write a child off because he or she seems too difficult, we may relinquish that child's only opportunity to be reached.

What follows are examples of two children who seemed unreachable before learning the skills of peacemaking.

Accepting the Challenging Child: Ben

Acceptance is like the fertile soil that permits a tiny seed to develop into the lovely flower it is capable of becoming—acceptance enables a person to actualize his or her potential. (Thomas Gordon, 179)

By the time Ben came to me in second grade, he had already gained a reputation as one of the more difficult children in our K-6 school of over five hundred children. In first grade he had literally stalked the halls, defying teachers who had attempted to discipline him, and running off when reprimanded. During his first two years, he spent many hours in the principal's office; and he was described as hyperactive, angry, oppositional, and unable to get along with his peers.

When I learned that Ben was going to be in my class, I wanted immediately to make him feel accepted. Discovering that Ben spent most of his time in the care of his grandmother, I decided to visit the two of them prior to the start of school. It was a hot August day when I stopped by as Ben played in front of the house and his grandmother watered the flowers.

"Hi, Ben," I said, "I just wanted to let you know you're going to be in my class this year. I want to welcome you and let you know how happy I am to have you with me."

He seemed surprised, didn't say much, and looked at me from time to time as though wondering if I were for real. Before long his grandmother and I began talking; she expressed concern and care for Ben, offering to help in any way she could. I assured her that Ben was going to have a great year and that I would be there for him in any way he needed. Ben just listened, but I noticed his face begin to soften.

On the first day of school I warmly welcomed Ben, referred to the conversation at his grandmother's house, and reiterated how happy I was to see him. I seated him in front of the room close to my desk, not just to "keep an eye on him," but so that I could be readily available for support and encouragement.

Very quickly I saw that Ben's hyperactivity and lack of focus were serious impediments to his learning, and that these problems were compounded by his low self-esteem. Ben's frustration would often result in fits of anger, exacerbated by his belief that the other children were watching him and making fun of his mistakes. Ben's problems came to a head during the second week of school. Let's look inside my classroom to see how a difficult situation became the window through which I could see Ben's problems more clearly.

Journal Entry: September 16

Early in the school year, I like to use a lesson called "Things I'm Good At," which helps to build self-esteem.

"Boys and girls," I began, "we're all good at certain things, and not so good at other things. For example, I'm good at drawing. When I was your age, I used to draw all the time; and even as a grown-up I still draw whenever I can." (I showed them a pen-and-ink drawing I had done.)

Next I shared that I was always bad at throwing and catching a ball, saying, "I used to be so embarrassed every time my class played baseball on the playground that I would look for any excuse not to play. But I also remembered that there were things I was good at, and that made me feel better."

"Every one of you is good at something, and today we're going to spend some time talking and writing about things you're good at, things that make you feel proud."

"What are some of the things you're good at? Turn to the person sitting across from you and answer this question together."

The paired sharing went on for a while; then the children shared in the large group. We talked at length; and their answers included being good at reading, sports, helping at home, riding a bike, cleaning their rooms, and taking care of pets. Some of the children who'd had trouble coming up with an idea realized that they were good at "caring" about family members, pets, or the world. By the end of the discussion every child had a topic to write about except Ben who had put his head down on the table and said nothing. I carefully approached him in an attempt to help him delve below the veneer of his poor self-image and discover at least one quality he felt good about.

Me: Ben, I bet there's something you're really good at.

Ben: Nothing. I'm not good at nothing.

Me: How could that be. You're a special person and I know you have things you're good at.

Ben (looking more negative): I told you, I'm not good at nothing.

Me (going on a hunch): I have a feeling you're good at caring.

Ben (picking up his head and shouting): I don't care about nobody, and nobody cares about me! (Obviously I had touched a nerve.)

Me: Is that how you feel, like nobody cares about you?

Ben: Yeah, nobody does.

Me: You're wrong there, Ben. Somebody does care about you, and I know who that person is for sure.

Ben: Who?

Me: It's me. I care about you. I like you and I care about you. (He looked at me in disbelief, but his eyes filled with tears.) And there's someone else I know cares about you, too.

Ben: Who's that?

Me: Your grandmother, that's who. I know she cares about you because she told me.

Ben (crying now): No she doesn't! She doesn't care about me at all!

Me (reflecting what I heard him saying): You feel that she doesn't care about you? I can see why you're feeling sad. But why do you feel that she doesn't care?

Ben: Because she's always too busy to talk to me when the other kids are around. (Ben's grandmother baby-sits a group of children).

Me (reflecting his feelings again): So you'd like more of her attention, and you feel that she doesn't give it to you because she doesn't care about you?

Ben (crying, shoulders shaking): She doesn't!

Me: Ben, I'm going to tell you a little secret. Your grandmother cares about you and loves you very much. She told me so, and I believe her. In fact, she even offered to come into the class to help on Fridays.

Ben (brightening a little): She did?

Me: She did. In fact, she offered to come in because she cares about you and wants you to have a good year—and so do I. (He stopped crying and looked at me) Would you like her to come in?

Ben: Yeah, I would.

Me: You do care about her, don't you?

Ben: I guess so.

Me: And she cares about you, too—a lot.

Ben: You think so?

Me: I know so. (Ben finally smiled). Now, how about writing something about caring for Nana. I bet you help her with the other kids. I have a feeling you're real good at that.

Ben: I do.

Me: That's a way of showing you care. You can write about that.

Ben: Will you help me.

Me: I'll help you.

Tentatively, Ben picked up his pencil and began writing. Before long he had a short paragraph starting with the words, "I'm good at helping my Nana. . . ."

Reflection

We, as teachers, must find a place in our hearts that enables us to love children like Ben. By doing so, we can better help them to love themselves. Thomas Gordon told us:

> . . . the genuine acceptance of a person, just as he or she is, is the critical factor in fostering that person's constructive change, in facilitating the person's problem solving, in encouraging movement toward greater psychological health or productive learning. It is a beautiful paradox of life that when people feel genuinely accepted by another as they are, they are free to think about how they want to develop, grow, change, be more of what they are capable of being. (179)

Looking at this episode with Ben, I can see how true Gordon's statement is. Receiving unconditional acceptance, coupled with firmness, limits, and expectations of success, Ben thrived. For the first time since starting school, he began functioning on grade level, stopped fighting with other children, and developed a deep appreciation for learning. In Part II you will see this reflected in Ben's writing. Acceptance was the key to his growth and change.

Learning to Rethink One's Actions: Juan

Peace cannot be kept by force. It can only be achieved by understanding. (Einstein)

Mastery in the emotional domain is especially difficult because skills need to be acquired when people are usually least able to take in new information and learn new habits of response—when they are upset. Coaching in these moments helps. Anyone, adult or fifth grader, needs some help being a self-aware observer when they're so upset. . . . (Daniel Goleman, 266-267)

Juan was a troubled sixth grader with a quick, violent temper. His teacher often sent Juan to my room to "help" the younger children and receive informal mentoring from me. I would frequently talk to him about whatever was on his mind, giving subtle guidance on how to handle his easily ignited anger. Sometimes Juan would stop by during lunch for an open ear, something that was sorely missing in his young life.

One day I heard Juan had gotten into serious trouble. He'd had a dispute in the lunchroom, shoving another student against the corner of a shelf. The child required stitches in the resulting gash, and Juan was suspended.

When the suspension was over, I called Juan to my room so I could hear firsthand what had happened. Since I wasn't able to coach him during the conflict, I decided to help him take another look at what had happened so he could avoid a recurrence. Our conversation went like this.

Me: I was sorry to hear you were suspended. What happened?

Juan: Me and Lev got into a fight and I pushed him.

Me: Is that why you were suspended?

Juan: Yeah, he was bleeding real bad and he had to go to the hospital.

Me: How did you feel about that?

Juan: Bad. I didn't mean to hurt him so bad. I just got angry, that's all.

Me: Juan, we've talked about your anger before; and you seemed to understand that you have to choose other actions when you get angry.

Juan: It just happened so fast, and Lev really got on my nerves.

Me: What did he do?

Juan: He kept messin' with me. He took my hat and I told him to give it back, but he wouldn't. So I tried to grab it and he kept pulling it away, so I finally grabbed him and shoved him. That's when he fell into the corner and cut his head.

Me (reflecting his feeling): Lev can be a tease, right?

Juan (balling his fist and punching it into his open palm): Yeah, he was really makin' me mad

Me: It sounds like you *were* real mad; but then you ended up getting in big trouble, so was it worth it?

Juan: Not really.

Me: What can you do next time you feel that angry, so you don't end up making a choice that gets you in trouble and harms the other person?

Juan: I don't know.

Me: Were there any adults around?

Juan: Yeah, there were. I guess I could have gone for help. (We had previously discussed this as an option).

Me: That would have been a great idea. Then maybe you could have avoided the fight. Did you try talking to Lev first?

Juan: I did. I tried giving him an "I message" (another option we had previously discussed). But he still didn't stop. He was really playin' with me.

Me (empathizing): It is frustrating when you try to give someone an "I message" and they don't listen. That makes me angry, too. But you have to remember, you always have a choice about your actions.

Juan: When I get mad like that, it's hard to think.

Me: I know what you mean. Remember how we talked about cooling off?

Juan: Oh, yeah. I guess I didn't do that.

Me: What were some of the things we talked about that you can do when you get angry?

Juan: I can get a drink of water or take some deep breaths.

Me: That's right. And you can get help after you do those things if you need to.

Juan: I'm gonna try to remember this stuff for next time. I don't wanna get suspended again and I don't wanna hurt someone bad like I did to Lev. I'm lucky he forgave me.

Reflections

How essential it is to teach our children mastery in the emotional domain. As Thomas Likona said, "It takes will to keep emotion under the control of reason." Teachers need to help young people build an internal discourse that guides their actions. Only by teaching specific skills can we enable our children to begin mastering their emotions. Until that time, they will respond automatically and without forethought when faced with anger and conflict. The only way to avoid this kind of response is to teach anger management/conflict resolution skills during a neutral time, a time when they are not embroiled in conflict. Teaching the skills in advance opens the way to coaching when an actual conflict occurs. In Juan's case if a trained adult had been nearby, the conflict may have been deflected. Juan would have been encouraged to cool off, and mediation could have ensued. This case shows the importance of doing peacemaking schoolwide. The more people in the school community trained in these skills, the greater the chance for their successful use.

CHAPTER Four

Integrating Peacemaking as the Year Goes On

As teachers our goal is greater than just passing on facts and information. If we want our students to be caring human beings, then we need to respond to them in caring ways. If we value our children's dignity, then we need to model the methods that affirm their dignity.

—Adele Faber and Elaine Mazlish, 42

Building Collaboration Through Learning

After being absorbed in peacemaking activities since the first day of school, children quickly begin the road toward self-management, becoming better able to handle decision-making. They also accrue skills that ameliorate potential conflicts before they even begin. A subtle sense of collegiality surfaces, and you, as teacher, can move more into the background as children start taking ownership of problem solving. After you have carefully laid the groundwork, your role in peacemaking becomes more of guide and facilitator rather than authority figure.

Allowing children to work in cooperative groups helps this process. In *Teaching Children Self-Discipline* Thomas Gordon wrote about the need for teachers to share power with their students. "Students need not depend only on the teacher. They can (and are urged to) depend a great deal on themselves, their own creativity and other members of their [cooperative] team. All this frees them from dependence on the teacher and, in doing so gives them both power and freedom" (141) . Beyond this point, children begin to take more responsibility for their own learning, formulating questions, seeking information, engaging in discourse with peers, and discovering new insights. Hence, the learning process and the social process are both enhanced. Once again look inside the classroom.

Collaborating During Math

Journal Entry: October 6

I'm noticing partnership and collaboration evolving spontaneously out of the peacemaking skills I teach and model every day. Author, workshop leader Carol Avery stresses the value of collaboration, saying, "Children learn from each other as well as from the enthusiasm, emphasis, attention, involvement, and expectation of the teacher" (qtd. in Bissex, 126). This is what's happening naturally; the children are taking an active role in their own learning, building collaborations along the way. Here's an example:

I've just taught a math lesson on place value in double-digit numbers, and the children have returned to their seats to complete a follow-up assignment. In most introductory activities, I have encouraged the children to work together and help each other. Lately I've noticed an interesting balance occurring: Children are discovering their strengths and weaknesses, seeking each other out accordingly. Right now, Kevin, who is very strong in math, is helping Max, Nick, Basil, and Tommy, who are not. They're sitting together at a table counting popsicle sticks bundled into tens and ones. Kevin shows his peers how to record the corresponding double-digit numbers on their worksheets. As I listen, I notice that Kevin affirms and encourages them along the way. "Basil's getting far on his paper," he exclaims as I walk by. He's genuinely happy that Basil's finally "getting it."

In fact the entire group is encouraging each other.

"Nick's getting even further than me," replies Basil. Nick beams.

"Hey, good job, Max," Tommy says with a smile. I smile too, just watching them.

Because we often work cooperatively throughout the day, the children have begun to create informal cooperative groups without my prompting.

Regardless of subject area, the children gravitate toward one another, helping, sharing, and offering support.

Cooperative Groups in Literature

Journal Entry: October 27

I have prepared the children for their first cooperative experience, teaching them to take turns speaking and to listen carefully to one another without interrupting. They have not been given specific roles, but they have been encouraged to combine their ideas for the purpose of creating puppet shows about *Pippi Longstocking*, the novel we've just completed. There are five different groups, all self-selected; and after about ten minutes, I noticed a number of children having problems with the delegation of roles and organization of tasks. I quickly chose group leaders for the groups having difficulty.

Amanda, leader of Group 5, approached me with a look of frustration . "This isn't working! Everyone has their own ideas and no one wants to do anyone else's."

Scott, a child in Amanda's group who always wants to do things his own way, came up to me next and said "Can I have another piece of paper? I don't want to do these ideas. I have a new one of my own."

I replied to Scott, "This is part of the problem Amanda's talking about."

Amanda, now angry, said, "I just want people to write their ideas down; then we can vote!"

Before I had a chance to respond, Mary Lynn from Group 3, edged her way between Scott and Amanda. "We're having a problem too, Mrs. Drew. Our group isn't cooperating."

I saw immediately that I'd have to do some troubleshooting. Holding up the quiet sign (two fingers up, just like the peace sign), I said to the class, "Let's all stop our groups and sit down together for a minute." All the groups joined me at the board. On it, I wrote the word "compromise."

Turning to the class, now seated on the floor before me, I asked, "What does this word mean?" We discussed the meaning of "compromise"; and as we did, I made sure it was clear to everyone that "compromise" means to give and take, and to be open to the ideas of others.

"Are you all willing, I ask the children , to compromise with others in your group and let go of some of your own ideas for the sake of working well with them?" Heads began to nod as they realized that was exactly what they needed to do.

"Remember, we won't be able to put together our puppet shows if we can't compromise," I added, before they returned to their groups.

Ten minutes later, Scott approached me excitedly. "We're finally getting a little more organized," he said with obvious satisfaction.

"What's changing?" I asked.

"We're each writing down our own parts and putting them together," Scott replied.

Prem, who had been listening to the whole thing, turned to me with an "Aha!" expression and said, "I think I'll write Scott an affirmation." He walked over to the Affirmation Box (page 42) as the animated sounds of children discussing *Pippi Longstocking* rose around the room like music.

Cooperation at Computers

Journal Entry: October 16

A problem arose during free-choice time today. So many children wanted to work on the three computers in the classroom that they were crowd-ing behind those who were already there, waiting for someone to leave, instead of choosing another center, as they are supposed to do if one is filled.

Alyssia approached me with a troubled expres-sion. "Mrs. Drew, too many kids are at the com-puter at the same time; and they don't want to share, so everybody's crowding."

Avoiding giving her a solution, I turned to Alyssia and said, "Sounds like a problem. What do you think can be done about it?"

Alyssia looked puzzled, thought hard for a minute and answered. "They need to take turns."

"That makes sense," I offered, "but how do you think that might happen?"

Alyssia's face brightened. "I have an idea," she said. "Let's sign up for the computer. That way everyone will know when their turn is." She walked over to the scrap box, found several pieces of lined paper, and fashioned three signs, one for each computer. Next, she walked over to the group with her signs and a pencil and told them about her idea. Apparently they liked it because they started putting their names on sign-up sheets.

Tommy came to me, irritated. "Mrs. Drew, I want to go to the computer too; but no one's getting up. Those kids have been on it for a while."

"They've signed up for a turn on the sign-up sheet Alyssia just made," I answered

"Yeah, but some of those games last so long. By the time the game's over it'll be too late for me to get a turn."

"Good point. What do you think we can do?" I asked.

"How about if each person gets ten minutes; then the next person can pick up where they left off on the game or start a new one."

"Let's give it a try," I said.

"Can I tell the class?" Tommy asked.

Sure," I replied, ringing the bell for the class's attention. The class stopped all activity when they heard the bell, their signal for immediate quiet. "Boys and girls, Tommy has an announcement," I told them.

Tommy began, "I got an idea. How about if we each have ten minute turns at the computer. That way more people can get a chance." He went on to explain his plan, and the class agreed to try it. Walking over to the chart Alyssia had made, he took a red marker and wrote at the top: "10 min. time limit."

Before long, the children resumed their activities, honoring the terms of the agreement they negotiated. The plan held all year long.

A Science Collaboration

Learning should not only take us somewhere; it should allow us later to go further more easily.
(Jerome Bruner, 17)

Journal Entry: November 10

We're studying rocks as part of a science unit on how the earth changes. The room is filled with books and posters about rocks, and our science table is so laden with rocks the children have brought in that I've had to set up another rock center. We've learned that rocks contain pigment, which can be used as color and dye; and on the playground today, Allison, Brittany, and Kristina find a large orange sandstone rock that they excitedly hauled into the classroom in search of pigment.

"Mrs. Drew, we think this rock might have pigment inside it. Look, it's all orange, and when we hold it the orange gets on our hands," said Allison, her eyes shining.

"What do you want to do with it?" I asked, resisting the impulse to give them my own suggestion.

"How about if we set up a pigment center by the sink. Maybe we can use the paint brushes and water to see if there's any pigment in the rock," said Kristina.

"How would you know if there was pigment? I wondered aloud.

"We can wet the brush; rub it on the rock; then try to paint with it at the easel. If it turns into paint, there must be pigment," Kristina stated, forming a logical hypothesis and conclusion.

"That sounds really interesting," I said. "Why don't you try it.

"Hey, we can put some of the pigment into this container and see if the water turns orange," Ben interjected excitedly, holding up a plastic beaker.

The group put on smocks and began their work. Other children passed by, asking questions as the group worked. Kevin brought a book opened to a page with photographs of sandstone. "Look," he said, this rock looks like the one you found on the playground." More children gathered round to see. The experiment continued, with children sharing materials and ideas, and this new "center" became one of the most popular in the class. By stepping back and allowing the children to share ideas, they put the process of peacemaking into action, including one another in collaboration, negotiating the use of materials, and working together peacefully. As a result, their learning is more dynamic, more their own.

More Reinforcement Techniques

You will want to find every opportunity you can to reinforce peacemaking. The more you do so, the more your students will absorb and apply the skills. What follows are some highly effective, easy reinforcement techniques that you can use repeatedly throughout the year.

Peacemaker of the Week

In my room is a bulletin board set up to last all year long. At the top are the words "Peacemaker of the Week" in bright, bold letters. Below is a large yellow sunshine in which photographs of the peacemakers will be placed weekly. To the left of the sunshine is a chart entitled, "A Peacemaker is Someone Who . . ." (see Chapter 1, page 0). To the right are the Win/Win guidelines, and around the sunshine are photographs of all the children.

On alternate Fridays we choose Peacemakers of the Week. We start by reviewing, "A Peacemaker is Someone Who . . ." together and then individually thinking about children in our class who have been peacemakers over the past two weeks. Each child then receives a ballot to vote for a peer who has best exhibited the qualities outlined on the chart. Votes are confidential and based on the qualities of a peacemaker, not on friendships and alliances. All ballots are placed in a bag labeled "Peacemaker of the Week."

Generally three or more children who receive the highest number of votes are named Peacemaker of the Week. No one wins a second time, though, until every child in the class has had a turn. What about the children who have had trouble meeting the criteria? I talk to them privately, offering coaching in the areas they need to work on, giving them

encouragement and support. The class knows they can vote for people who have made large improvements, even though they may still have some difficulty meeting the criteria completely.

The Peacemakers of the Week get gold ribbons to wear and certificates to take home. The words appear on the certificate: *"Each person has the ability to affect the world around us. We congratulate you for affecting our world in a positive way."*

After the certificates are awarded, children in the class can affirm each peacemaker, and then affirm each other. I usually have all the children turn to a person sitting next to them, positioning their bodies so that they can look at their partner's face. Next I have them think of something kind to say to that person, something that relates to a positive attribute. Gianna says to Kristen, "I like the way you always share your markers with me. You're a kind person." This way everybody gets affirmed, not just the peacemakers of the week.

I always keep careful records of who receives this award, making sure every child does so before anyone wins a second time. I have never had a child not earn this award, at least for improvement. Through our support, teachers can help even the most difficult students get to this point.

Peacemaking Journals

Journals can be an excellent reinforcement for peacemaking as well as writing. From time to time you can have children take a few moments to reflect upon peacemaking lessons they have learned in school, and ways they have integrated these lessons into their lives. The following ideas can be used over and over again in journals. You'll find each time students write about any of the following topics they will do so with a different perspective.

- A recent conflict I've had, and how I resolved it.
- A conflict I've had that wasn't resolved; possible solutions.

- A conflict I've observed. What happened? Was it resolved? Why or why not? If it was unresolved, what prevented the resolution? Can you think of a way of resolving it?
- Conflicts in literature. (Use the above questions to analyze it.
- Ways I am a peacemaker.
- Ways I want to improve as a peacemaker.
- Peacemakers in my life.
- Peacemakers in literature.
- Peacemakers in the news.
- Accepting others: Is there someone I have trouble accepting? Why? What can I do about this?
- Prejudice? What is it? Do I see prejudice in my life? How do I feel about this?
- How can I help make the world a more peaceful place?
- Kindness: What acts of kindness have I done recently?
- How can I become a more peaceful person?
- Am I a peacemaker within my own family?
- When I am an adult, how can I continue to be a peacemaker?

Affirmation Box

When we affirm, we simply pay a sincere compliment to another person. This process engenders care among members of a class and builds individuals' self-esteem, which create an atmosphere of safety and acceptance. Affirmations that children offer to each other enable them to work together more harmoniously, thus strengthening the foundation of your peaceful classroom. Affirmations can be spoken or written. Children who shy away from writing often won't hesitate to write lengthy affirmations for people they care about. Now, step into my classroom to see the affirming technique in action.

Journal Entry: November 7

We started an Affirmation Box today. Gianna and Tahvia covered an old shoe box with wrapping paper; I cut a slot in the top; and wrote on it in large black letters: AFFIRMATION BOX. I told the children they could affirm each other at any time by taking a paper from the pad next to the box and writing a note of acknowledgement for anyone in the class. They loved the idea, and we spent time talking about the kinds of things they might want to write. Oral affirmations where children compliment each other for positive attributes are a constant part of our class, and written affirmations take the process a step further, enabling the children to use their growing writing skills at the same time.

Jennifer often helps Nick with his assignments. She takes the time to explain things he has trouble understanding and patiently answers his frequent questions. As I passed Nick's seat today, I overheard him say to Dominic, "Help me spell terrific. I want to write an affirmation for Jennifer." This is a big step for Nick. He usually hates to write.

Another way to use the Affirmation Box is to have each child pick another child's name out of a hat, writing an affirmation to the child whose name they have picked. I actually prefer this method since it avoids the possibility of a child being left out, but it's important to prepare the children thoroughly for it. One way is to have them sit in a circle. Go around the circle and tell each child three positive things you've noticed about her or him. Then have the class walk around for a moment. Each time you flick the lights every child must stand next to the closest person and think of one positive thing to say. Help the children focus on positive attributes you have observed in each of them: academic strengths; physical abilities; and positive character traits like helpfulness, sharing, caring, and listening. If anyone has trouble thinking of affirmations for their partners, help them.

You can carry this method a step further by having the children pick names of classmates out of a hat and then writing an "Affirmation Story" to that child. When I've done this with my class,

I've given them the following prompts to help them get started.

- What is something nice you've noticed about this person?
- What is this person good at? Describe in detail.
- What other positive things have you noticed about this person?
- Are there any ways you would like to be like this person?
- Is there anything you can learn from this person?

You can have each child draw a picture of the person they are writing about to go along with the Affirmation Story. You will find that children treasure these stories and save them to read when they need a lift.

Don't forget the simple act of affirming the children yourself. "Gianna, you're so kind and helpful. "Max, you're concentrating so well on your work; I'm proud of you." Words like these

can make a child's day and bolster spirits. It helps children see their own positive traits and behaviors. Affirming your students also sets an example for them to affirm each other.

Breakdowns

Do things always go smoothly when peacemaking is taught? Absolutely not!—as the following journal entries clearly indicate. Peacemaking skills ultimately helped pull things back together in each of these situations; but life is imperfect, and sometimes negative situations arise no matter how many skills we know.

Temporary Pandemonium

Journal Entry: September 16

Today started off well, but at clean-up for dismissal things started to go awry. We were running late, so I let all the children pack up at once, rather than calling them by table as I usually do. Mistake! As they all scurried at once to pack their bookbags, the resulting din obliterated the calmness and order I had worked so hard to achieve from the first day of school. Tommy and Teddy started chasing each other along the side of the room, as Erica sat on the floor surrounded by the week's worth of papers she'd pulled out of her cubby (why now?!!), unsure of which to pack first; and Max wandered about the room, crying because he couldn't find his lunchbox. At this point, Basil started whooping like an ape and Sam, eyes glazed over, sat on the floor in the midst of the pandemonium and tuned it out.

"Help!" I yelled in my head, wondering how I could possibly regain control of my class *and* get everyone out the door in the three minutes remaining before the bell rang.

I took a deep breath and held up my hand in the (usually very effective) Quiet Sign. "QUIET SIGN," I projected in my loudest *nonshouting* voice. A few voices lowered.

"QUIET SIGN," I repeated, trying to look perfectly calm and in control, my feelings notwithstanding. A few more voices lowered; then a few hands raised along with mine, signaling the Quiet Sign to others.

One more time, in a lowered voice, I repeated, "Quiet Sign." This time every hand went up with mine and every voice finally quieted.

"That took *too* long, boys and girls," I said firmly but calmly. "Next time I expect everyone to listen this fast," I said, snapping my fingers. The children nodded their heads.

"How fast?" I asked.

"This fast!" they responded, snapping their fingers, as they sat quietly on the floor, peaceful once again, save Max who quietly whimpered over his still-missing lunchbox.

My lesson: This class cannot be rushed. There's so much innate energy in so many of the children that a simple breakdown in our routine can bring all the energy tumbling out at once. Also, I need to remind myself that peacemaking isn't a panacea; it doesn't ameliorate every problem. I always need to remember to tune in to the children, to anticipate their needs, and to manage time well, even when we're running late.

Postlude

Our daily routines go smoother now and we've had no more catastrophes at dismissal time. I'm seeing that this class needs plenty of time for transitions, and attempts to rush them create tension and anxiety—exactly what they don't need.

The kids are taking more and more responsibility now, not only with work but also with book sign-out, room clean-up, and organizational tasks. When we prepared to go home today, the scenario had changed from two weeks ago.

Mary Lynn ran up to me, smiling, and said, "Teddy was just so helpful. He asked if he could put up my chair for me." (This was not an assigned job, just something he decided to do on his own.)

Now I noticed Max (perpetually disorganized) turning to Teddy and saying, "Can you help me find my coat?"

Teddy patiently replied, "In a minute, Max. I need to ask the kids something." He turned to the class; asked for their attention; and spoke to all of them in a clear, direct voice, "I need help putting up chairs."

Kevin got up to help. Others followed. Soon all the chairs were up; Max had found his coat; and we were ready for dismissal *with two whole minutes to spare.*

Fighting

Conflict is a natural part of our lives. Conflicts arise over misunderstandings, unmet needs, different values and perceptions. Children can be taught to deal constructively with conflicts. When channeled into positive action, conflict stimulates creativity and problem-solving ability. (Fram Schmidt, iii)

Journal Entry: September 17

Both Tommy and Teddy have a history of acting out; in fact, Max still bears a scar above his right eye from the time Teddy struck him in the head with a block when they were in kindergarten. Since the start of school, they've been teasing, calling each other names, and fighting. Their "baggage" from home, natural mischeviousness, and strong need to express frustration, ran counter to their desire to be peacemakers. After sending them both to the principal's office this morning, I called Tommy's mother and set up a meeting with Teddy's father. I had a very forceful conversation with both boys when they returned from the principal's office.

"Guys," I said, "guess you've begun to notice that I'm not going to tolerate any nonsense from either of you. I know you've been getting away with things at home because your parents told me so, but it's not going to happen here. You have two choices. You can either choose to behave when you're in school, and by that I mean listen to the people who care about you, and work out your conflicts instead of fighting, or you can choose to do the opposite, in which case you're going to be spending a lot of time with your heads down, missing free time, or in the principal's office. It's up to you."

They both agreed that the former would be preferable.

I also decided to mediate today's conflict, hoping to get to the bottom of whatever was setting off the two of them.

Me: Tommy, look at Teddy and tell him what you're upset about.

Tommy (looking at me): Teddy punched me, so I had to hit him back.

Me: Tell Teddy, not me; and start from "I."

Tommy (looking at Teddy): I'm really angry because you punched me. That's why I punched you back.

Me: Teddy, say back to Tommy what you heard him say. (This very deliberate step is important for two reasons: [1] paraphrasing opens up a person's willingness to listen and [2] reflective listening builds empathy.)

Teddy (looking at Tommy): I heard you say that you're angry at me because I punched you, and that's why you punched me back.

Tommy: That's right. You shouldn't have punched me.

Me: Punching's not allowed. You both know that. Teddy, give Tommy an I message to let him know what's bothering you.

Teddy: You always annoy me.

Me: Start from "I," Teddy.

Teddy: I don't like it when you annoy me. It makes me mad.

Me: Tommy, say back what Teddy just said.

Tommy: You get mad when I annoy you.

Me: It's ok to get mad, but is it ok to punch?

Teddy (looking down, embarrassed): No.

Me: What can the two of you do instead of punching next time you get mad?

Tommy (frustrated): It's not gonna matter what Teddy says because he always punches.

Me (realizing Tommy may be right): Teddy, you do hit and punch the other kids a lot. Even with all our peacemaking you're still doing it. Does somebody treat you that way?

Teddy reddened, looked down at the floor, and grew silent. I felt I'd touched a nerve. I decided to pursue it, but I was prepared to back off if Teddy resisted even slightly.

Me: Is there somebody who punches you or hurts you, Teddy?

Teddy looked up at me with a troubled expression. Then he blurted: It's my big brother! He's 14. He punches me all the time, and he beats me up whenever my father isn't around. Every time I tell my father he [my brother] stops for a little while, but then he just starts again. No matter what I do, he still punches me.

Me: So you punch other people like your brother punches you.

Teddy: Yeah, I guess I do. I hate when he does that to me. He punches me every day!

Tommy: But that doesn't mean you should punch me!

At this point I realize more intervention may be needed. I decided to speak to our guidance counselor at the end of the day and to call Teddy' father as well. I'm not sure if he's aware of how often Teddy's being attacked by his big brother.

Me: There are other ways to handle your anger, Teddy. You don't have to be like your brother. I'm going to be meeting with you father tomorrow, and I'm going to talk with him about what's been going on. Maybe he can get your brother to stop punching you.

Teddy: I hope so.

Me: But in the meantime, what can you do instead of punching the next time you get mad?

Teddy: I can give the person an "I message" or go for help.

Me: Please try that, Teddy. I know you don't want to keep getting in trouble. Tommy, how about you? Instead of hitting back, what can you do?

Tommy: Cool off and tell an adult.

Me: Remember that, Tommy. Remember also, guys, that you're both friends , and you don't want to lose the friendship—right?

Teddy: Your right, Mrs. Drew, but it's gonna be hard.

Me: Come to me, Teddy, whenever you feel like you're going to punch. I believe that'll help. Teddy agreed and the boys shook hands.

Journal Entry: February 18

It's been six months since the day Tommy and Teddy had their last fight. Although they've both needed extra guidance and frequent support, they have absorbed the skills of peacemaking and have been finding ways to work out their differences. Staying in touch with their parents has helped, as has continuous affirmation for good behavior.

I reminded Teddy about using peacemaking skills with his brother at home. It seems that his brother had started hitting him again, but Teddy admitted that he often instigated it by annoying his brother. He agreed to do some win/win strategies the next time a conflict came up.

Journal Entry: February 28

Things seem to be getting better between Teddy and his brother. Teddy announced today that his brother hadn't hit him at all this week. "I've been using 'I messages,'" he said proudly. I hope he keeps it up, for I see what he's accomplished with Tommy. (They're still resolving their conflicts with words, not fists.)

A Triangle

Amanda, Erica, and Jennifer had been "best friends" since kindergarten. By now, though, the three-way friendship was wearing thin. Their complaints after recess were growing more frequent, and a pattern of negative triangulation had developed. Although mediations are generally done with only two disputants at a time, after several unsuccessful attempts at working with the girls in pairs, I decided to try mediating with all three present.

Me: Girls, I'm getting tired of hearing these complaints about each other every day.

Amanda: Well Erica won't let me and Jennifer play together. She keeps coming over and bothering us.

Erica: But I want to play with Jennifer too.

Jennifer: It's OK with me if Erica plays with us.

Erica: But Amanda always says "no."

Amanda: Sometimes I want to play with Jennifer myself. Why does Erica always have to play with us?

Erica: I don't have anyone else to play with.

Me: Sounds like you have a big problem, girls. This has been going on for a while.

Amanda: Well, if Erica would just leave us alone, we wouldn't have a problem.

Erica: But I want to play too.

Me: Jennifer, how do you feel about Erica's joining in?

Jennifer: Fine, but whenever I play with Amanda, she wants to go on the seesaw; and there's only room for two.

Me (encouraging them to come up with their own solution): Girls, how do you think you can solve this problem, once and for all?

Amanda: I think Erica should make some new friends.

Me: Instead of focusing on Erica, what can *you* do, Amanda? (She shrugged.)

Jennifer: I think the three of us should try to play together like we used to.

Erica: But Amanda always seems to get mad at me.

Me: Amanda, I think you need to take a little responsibility here. What can you do differently?

Amanda: I guess I can let Erica play, but then we always end up not getting along.

Me: That seems to be the case. You know sometimes it's OK to agree not to play together.

Jennifer: Maybe instead of all of us playing together we can take turns . . . one day I'll play with Amanda and one day I'll play with Erica.

Me (turning to Erica and Jennifer): Girls, what do you think?

Erica: OK, I'll try it.

Me: Amanda?

Amanda: (somewhat reluctantly): I guess.

Me: Are you all willing to treat each other respectfully when you're not playing together, no put-downs or faces at each other? (They nodded yes.) Would you like to shake on it? (They shook hands and returned to their seats. The solution has held.)

Reflections On Dealing with Breakdowns

In each of the foregoing cases, problems occurred that were eventually solved. The foundation for peacemaking had been set ahead of time, serving as a scaffold for problem solving.

In the first scenario, poor time management on my part created tension that set the children off. By falling back on well-maintained listening skills, prompted by the Quiet Sign, a chaotic situation was kept under control, and calmness restored.

Scaffolding played a part in the second scenario as well. Here, Tommy and Teddy had not yet given up fighting habitually in spite of their cognitive grasp of peacemaking skills. Because we had previously role-played with puppets and showcased other people's conflicts, the boys were aware of better choices they could make when angry. Their ingrained automatic modes of response were still in play, however.

Their foundation in peacemaking, reinforced by daily modeling, eventually helped Teddy and Tommy become better choice-makers, affording them the realization that fighting doesn't solve anything. This view was strongly reinforced by my insistence that they adhere to our standard, "Fighting is not allowed." Because of their infraction, the boys had to go to the principal's office and have their parents contacted; thus Tommy and Teddy saw that the school stands behind its standards. The defining moment occurred, however, during conflict mediation when it became clear that Teddy had been transferring aggression from home to school. Finally we could address the root problem and help alleviate it.

Sometimes peacemaking results in the knowledge that certain combinations of friendships do not work. In the case of Amanda, Erica, and Jennifer, it was necessary to dissolve the unworkable triangle they had formed. Three-way friendships are difficult, and this one clearly wasn't working. The girls realized they could no longer all three play together. By deciding to pair off and alternate their play days, they found a workable solution. In more severe situations, children

often agree to keep away from each other, a more far more responsible decision than continually locking horns. A difficult but valuable lesson of peacemaking is that not all people can be friends, but we all can treat others with respect, even those people we don't care for.

Children Mentoring Each Other

One of the best ways for children to grasp peacemaking firmly is by teaching it to others. When children have this opportunity, they see themselves as role models and rise to the occasion. Prior learning is reinforced as new understanding takes place. Here's an example.

Journal Entry: December 7

A colleague's special education class came into our room to learn peacemaking from my students. My class was so excited at the prospect of sharing their growing knowledge and assuming the role of teacher. Many of the children in the visiting class had had difficulty with conflict, so we decided to talk about what kids can do when they get angry rather than choosing to fight. My class was right on target with their "expert" guidance. Here are their suggestions.

"Cool off if you're really mad."

"Take deep breaths."

"Drink some water."

"Walk away and calm down. Then go and talk to another person."

Both classes talked about cooling-off techniques at length, admitting how hard it is for all of us to take a step back when we're angry. But everyone agreed that it's essential to do exactly that.

We also focused on the rewards of making positive choices, and the consequences of making negative choices. "Boys and girls," I asked," if you get really angry and you make a positive choice like cooling off and talking it over instead of hitting, how do you feel about that afterwards?"

"I feel so much better," said Jennifer. "It makes me feel good about myself."

"I feel like I won't lose a friend," said Teddy.

"I feel like people like me better," said Collin.

"My parents are proud of me when I cool off instead of fighting with my little brother," said Kristen, "then I feel proud of myself!"

"How about if you choose to hit or punch or do something negative when you get angry," I asked. "How do you feel then?"

"I feel disappointed in myself, like I shouldn't have acted that way," answered Dominic.

"I know what you mean," said Chris, "I feel like I gave in to the bad feelings."

At this point Tommy, who'd been deep in thought, added, "Usually I feel bad because I know I'm not being a peacemaker; but sometimes I feel good, like when Teddy punched me."

"Why did you feel good?" I asked.

"Because I wanted to get even," Tommy replied frankly.

"But what happened after that?" I asked, remembering the situation.

"I got in big trouble, and I had to go to the principal's office; and my mom had to come to school, and then she punished me too."

"So was it worth it to get even?" I asked.

"Not at all," said Tommy.

By now all the children were completely animated. My students in the role of mentor were brimming with information to share, and the other class was relieved to have discovered that other people experienced the same kinds of problems they did.

The culmination was a discussion about things kids could do to have a more peaceful school, and both classes came up with the following ideas.

"Don't use put-downs."

"Treat other people with respect."

"Remember that people are the same on the inside even if they are different on the outside."

"Have a caring heart."

Through activities like this, children have another opportunity to examine decisions they have made, and to choose a new path in the future. Informal mentoring is beneficial to those who give it as well as those who receive. It provides another forum in which children of varied ages and abilities can connect and work together to create a more peaceful school.

Looking at the World Around Us

Peacemaking forms a lens through which children can view their world. In sharp contrast to the scenes depicted on TV and in videos, the world we represent through the lens of peacemaking shows positive alternatives, ethical choices, and hopeful possibilities.

Children desparately need this alternate vision.

Through the lens of peacemaking, children are not encouraged to ignore the negatives in life, pretending they don't exist; conversely, they are asked to deal with problems head on and to search for solutions. Peacemaking is a dynamic, proactive process wherein people take responsibility for the world around them, seeking ways to make things better.

Journal Entry: April 6

Lately we've been talking about the world around us and how peacemaking has the potential to make it a better place. The children's concerns about violence clearly came out in this discussion and their ensuing writing, as shown in the following samples.

Why This World Needs Peacemaking

This world needs peacemaking so there will be no more violence and no fighting. If there was fighting, everybody would be hurt. This world needs peacemaking so everybody will not be hurt and no one is in the hospital. To be a peacemaker you cool off, say an I message, say back.

—by Sara

I think we need to have peacemaking because people will start bringing guns and weapons and keep their anger and somebody might get killed or hurt. If there were peacemaking, the world would be a peaceful place and everyone would be happy inside. They would feel very peaceful.

—by Max

If we didn't have peacemaking the world will be a garbage can with dead people laying in it. If we had peacemaking we wouldn't be in a garbage can. Kids should be peacemakers, and other people should be too.

—by Nick

In going over the class's writing several times, I was shocked to note that *every child in the class* mentioned violence. Doing peacemaking in school gives children a sense of hope and faith that there's something people can do about it.

As the Year Comes to an End

Journal Entry: May 10

Today we talked and wrote about how important it is to apply peacemaking skills in all areas of our lives, acknowledging that this isn't always easy. Erica initiated a discussion by bringing up a frustration she often experiences with her sister.

"I told my sister to stop taking things, and I gave her an "I message"; but she wouldn't listen," she began, wth a perplexed expression.

Mary Lynn, who clearly identified with Erica, chimed in. "Sometimes my brother just ignores me when I try to work things out with him."

Remembering how often this problem is raised, I empathized. "I know how frustrating that can be. It's happened to me, too. Not everyone's learned how to be peacemakers like you have, so sometimes you need to show them how to do it by example. Don't give up because by

using peacemaking with others, you're teaching them how to do the same. Sometimes you have to be willing to take the first step even if the other person doesn't catch on right away. Eventually they will."

"But it's hard when my sister doesn't listen to me. How can I make her listen?" asked Erica, still searching for an answer.

"You can talk to her at a neutral time, a time when you're not angry with each other. Ask her to sit down with you and tell her what you just told me. Let her know that you want to get along better with her, and teach her how to use 'I messages' too."

"I'm gonna have to try that with my brother," said Mary Lynn, " 'cause he never listens to me."

"You can invite your mom to sit down with you and help, but don't do it in a tattling kind of way. Let her know you need help in talking to your brother and that the best way she can help is by asking him to just plain listen to you," I told her, understanding the frustration she has as the youngest in her family.

It's hard to be the one who stands on the firm ground of respect when others try to erode that ground with disrespect. Using put-downs, ignoring, fighting, ridiculing, and withdrawl all arise from the win/lose paradigm. Peacemaking skills prepare children to enter a new paradigm, one in which people seek solutions, work in concert, *struggle against a common problem rather than against each other*, and find win/win solutions. Mary Lynn and Erica expressed the same frustrations many children do when dealing with people uninitiated in the skills of peacemaking. Those who know these skills are the pathfinders. They must lead others into the new paradigm through their example.

Peace Starts with Us

The children are beginning to understand that if we want to have a peaceful world, it has to start with each of us. The following story, by Jennifer, reflects the difficulties and rewards of this process.

How I Use Peacemaking with My Friends and Family

My friend Elizabeth always looked in my private things. That got on my nerves. I thought she was old enough to know how to tell how I felt on my face. She did not know yet. So I told her how I felt. She listened but she didn't obey. I was very angry at her. I said, "You are one of my friends, but you are making me madder than mad!" She said, "OK, just this once I will listen to you." I was a little surprised for a long, long, extra long time. Then we had a cold drink and some food. I was full of happiness again. So we played and rested and did "I messages." Then we went in the pool.

—by Jennifer

I enjoyed the nuances of this story, especially the part where Jennifer said, "I thought she was old enough to know how to tell how I felt on my face. She did not know yet." How many adults get angry, as Jennifer did, thinking the other person (particularly one's spouse) should be able to read our feelings? At a young age, these children are learning the realities of human dynamics. May they take this knowledge into their adult lives and have better relationships as a result.

Seeing the Broader Implications

By now the children are clearly aware of their responsibility to live the skills of peacemaking. Many see their connection to the larger world as well. In the transformational work of peacemaking we must never lose that link. Peace starts with each of us; our individual actions affect our schools, communities, and the world in general. This theme has begun to come out in the children's writing and discussions.

Kevin wrote a story that reflects his growing understanding of the broader implications of peacemaking. He is one of the children who sees the link between individual acts and the larger world. I hope all of my students will eventually be able to grasp this link, because it is the essence of peacemaking.

If there wasn't peacemaking there would be a lot of violence. Peacemaking is a good thing. If people didn't believe in peacemaking there would be robberies, stealing, and hurting people. I hope people are being peacemakers. If we didn't have peacemaking a lot of people would get injured. I am going to be a peacemaker until I die.

—by Kevin

Journal Entry: June 3

Wanting to find out if and how the children had perceived changes within themselves, I assigned the following writing topic, "How I've Changed as a Human Being This Year." Tommy's and Chris' stories speak for many of them.

I used to go to the principal's every day and now I don't go to the principal's. Maybe because I'm using peacemaking and I'm doing better in school. I never knew how to use I messages and now I do. I messages are keeping me out of fights.

—by Tommy

This year I changed by being a good reader, less nervous, and a little more patient. Once I saw a fight held in the park. Two of my friends had a big problem because my other friends were playing with me, not them. So I said to them, "If you don't play with all of us, then I'm not playing." So I solved it out. Also I've changed by being a better listener. I've been a good listener by listening to other people when they speak, and the teachers, of course. I also have been a better helper to others by doing good things.

—by Chris

So many changes have occurred: Nick has learned that he can love his toy guns, but still be a peaceful person. Teddy's and Tommy's aggressiveness have all but disappeared. And, Chris— told you himself how he's changed. The most salient change of all is the deepened sensitivity among all the children toward one another and the world they live in.

In the words of Krista McAuliffe, the first teacher in space (1986), "I touch the future. I teach." As I think about the children in my class and many others whose lives have been touched by peacemaking, I feel privileged, knowing that the work I do each day helps to shape the future of our society and the world.

CHAPTER Five

Taking Care of Ourselves

Peace is present right here and now, in ourselves and in everything we do and see. The question is whether or not we are in touch with it. We don't have to travel far away to enjoy the blue sky. We don't have to leave our city or our neighborhood to enjoy the eyes of a beautiful child. Even the air we breathe can be a source of joy.

—Thich Naht Hanh, 5

Setting a Peaceful Tone Within

When I wrote *Learning the Skills of Peacemaking* (1983), I was a single mother raising my two boys alone and trying to survive financially on grants. It was one of the most exhilarating yet stressful times I can remember. I clearly recall reading a poem by a young girl from Israel who talked about "living in the land of peace where there is no peace." Her words resonated and their familiarity made me realize that figuratively I was doing a similar thing: trying to create a "land of peace" when, in fact, I had very little peace of my own.

My world was filled with responsibilities, obligations, and pressures. I had no time for myself, and when I did I was too tired to do anything but fall onto my sofa. I realized then that if I intended to write about peace, I would have to learn to live it. But how? I couldn't change the structure of my life, nor could I shed any of my responsibilities. If I couldn't feel a sense of peace within myself, how could I be peaceful with others? And if I couldn't create peace within

myself, how could I possibly help create it anywhere else?

I believed the answer lay in something outside of myself—more time, more money, a vacation. But the more I read and researched the book, the more I discovered there is a key to peace and—it's inside me.

Shifting the Mindset

In Victor Frankl's classic, *Man's Search for Meaning*, he told of his long-term confinement in a concentration camp. Frankl described how, in the horror of Auschwitz and other Nazi concentration camps, he was able to find resolution and peace within his own spirit. Frankl came to realize that the key to peace was not in the circumstances around him, but in how he chose to view the circumstances of his life.

> We who lived in the concentration camps can remember the men who walked through the huts comforting others, giving away their last piece of bread. They may have been few in

number, but they offer sufficient proof that everything can be taken from man but one thing: . . . to choose one's attitude in any given set of circumstances, to choose one's own way.

"To choose one's own way." What could I choose to do differently? My life certainly had all the important attributes: the people I loved were alive and healthy; I had a comfortable home, meaningful work, wonderful children, supportive friends. I knew I had to make a major shift in my thinking and acting, enabling myself to "choose my way" differently.

At that point I came across a book called *One Minute for Myself* in which Spencer Johnson advised taking one minute at a time randomly throughout the day to ask, "What is it I most need right now?" The premise was that by taking care of ourselves in simple ways, we feel uplifted and nurtured; and when this happens, we interact more peacefully with those around us.

Our momentary needs are often simple and easy to satisfy. For me, stopping what I was doing and staring at the trees outside my window, or drinking a calming cup of tea, or closing my eyes for a moment and taking slow deep breaths made a marked difference in my attitude. By taking care of myself in the moment, respecting my own needs, I experienced a shift in my general outlook. Simple acts like pulling off to the side of the road to look at the sky on a beautiful day or writing in my journal made a discernible difference. When I allowed myself those simple pleasures, I felt more loving and open toward the people around me; when I was overstressed I felt disconnected from others.

By taking one minute when I needed to, I was honoring myself, and thereby enabling myself to honor others. It became clear that being good to me was a prerequisite for any peacemaking work I would do.

How about you? How well do you treat yourself? As teachers we have one of the most demanding jobs in the world. Teachers nurture many other people, but who nurtures us? Right now stop and ask yourself, what kind and loving things can I do for myself each day?

What makes you feel calm and peaceful? Start a list of all the simple things you can start doing that will make a definable difference in the quality of your day. One teacher I know keeps special low-fat snacks in her desk; another puts on Mozart the minute the kids leave the classroom. I keep a jug of fresh spring water by my desk at all times. Sipping it throughout the day refreshes me.

Decide what you're going to do to honor yourself. Remember, you deserve this treatment, and also remember never to leave work at the end of the day without first looking up at the sky and breathing in the fresh air.

Replacing the Critical Voice with a Nurturing One

In *Celebrate Your Self*, Briggs talked about this principle, updating an old adage: "You will do unto others as you do unto yourself."

She said, "If you do not value your own Being, you cannot cherish others. Improving your relationship to yourself is where the action is. The treasure you seek lies within you" (4). Briggs is a strong proponent of "self-affirmation," the practice of giving yourself positive, empowering messages and speaking to yourself supportively. Her writings lead me to an awareness of a "critical parent" lodged in my head that compounded the stress in my life. The voice of the critical parent would often say negative things to me: "You lost that important letter. What's wrong with you? Can't you get more organized!" Or, "You're behind schedule with your writing. You should be more on top of things." The voice of the critical parent was harsh and debilitating— a heavy burden. It made me feel as though I could never measure up to the goals I had set.

When I became aware of the effects of the critical inner voice, I started making a conscious effort to replace it with one that was loving, nurturing, and accepting. Often throughout the day I would offer myself support by silently saying, "You're doing such a great job; I'm proud of you." At first it felt strange, but I quickly realized that I was empowering and energizing myself by saying kind things to myself. Life is difficult enough; we don't need to compound that fact by berating ourselves. As I became less ensnared in a web of critical messages, I felt freer, lighter, and more able to reach the goals I had set.

Take a moment and think about the messages you give to yourself. Is the voice in your head supportive or critical? If you're like I used to be, try to catch yourself each time your inner voice says something negative; and turn the negative message into a supportive one. You'll see how this process can make a huge difference in your outlook. A teacher I know who tried this, said, "I've become more patient with my students now that I'm more accepting of myself." Another teacher said, "I had no idea how hard I was being on myself. It was habitual. Now that I've freed up the energy I once use to put myself down, I feel happier and more effective."

Now think about the children you teach. How many already have internalized negative voices? You likely know children like a little boy I taught a few years back, who used to say "I can't" when faced with even a small challenge. At age six, the voice of failure had already become ingrained. Slowly, after a year of positive messages in school, he started to find the "I can" lurking beneath the "I can't." Through awareness, sensitivity, and affirmation, we can quiet negative voices, holding up a new mirror to each child and that reveals to ourselves the face of possibility.

Choosing Our Behaviors

Just as you are free to choose happiness over unhappiness, so in the myriad events of everyday life you are free to choose self-fulfilling behavior over self-defeating behavior. (Wayne Dyer, 18)

There was a time when I would find myself "tensing up" before the day even started. I would jump out of bed with a list in my head, rushing myself and my children through morning routines, then barreling out the door with one eye on the clock. When I understood that the way I handled circumstances, not the circumstances themselves, held power over my life, things started to change. I began to slow down, getting up a little earlier, writing in my journal before my children awakened, then playing a relaxing tape as I dressed. As I began to feel calmer, my sons did too; and I started to see that I really did have more control over my time than I had believed.

Realizing how essential physical exercise was to my well-being, I started carving out short periods of time each week to work out. Around the same time, I began saying daily affirmations (while I drove to work each day), picturing my affirmations manifesting as I said them. "I feel calm and relaxed throughout the day." "I'm in great physical shape." By focusing on what I wanted rather than what I did not want, I took a more proactive, empowering stance. Positive thoughts lead to positive behaviors; positive behaviors reinforced positive thoughts. As Hanh wrote, "By taking good care of the present moment, we take good care of the future. Working for peace in the future is to work for peace in the present moment" (38). By choosing nurturing thoughts and balanced actions, I took a big step toward peace in the present moment. Only then could I truly put my energies into the work required for peace for others.

The same holds true for you. The peacefulness you want to bring to your classroom has to start within yourself. What changes do you need to make in your own life to feel calm and centered? Do you need to re-examine your daily routines and make some adjustments, as I did? If the answer is "yes," start now.

As you begin to feel more peaceful within, it will be easier to bring this feeling to your

The Balm of Silence

Do you ever notice how noisy and turbulent life is? How often do you get to experience moments of exquisite calmness and simplicity? For some of us the only real quiet time we have is in the car; but that's still not the blank, unfettered time we need to access a true feeling of calmness. In order for the mind to experience peace, it needs times of complete quiet in which to reflect, let go, and relax. Yet we're surrounded with constant turbulence, which most of us have readily absorbed.

Deepak Chopra often talks about how essential silence is in our lives. Think about the children you teach. Are their lives flooded with the noise of loud voices, TV's, radios, and video games? Do they know what it is to lie in the grass and look at the sky, accompanied only by the sound of the breeze? A good friend of mine once said, "Our children have lost the simple art of daydreaming, and so have we." She was right. Our frenetic lives have begun to mirror the dissonant energy of our society.

Silence and the capacity to daydream need not be lost forever. If we make a conscious effort, we can bring these essential elements back into our lives. Chopra also said, "Practicing silence means making a commitment to take a certain amount of time to simply Be. It also means periodically withdrawing from the activity of speech . . . watching television, listening to the radio . . ." (14). This practice enables us to feel more peaceful and opens our channels of creativity. What a gift we will give to ourselves by the simple act of indulging in brief periods of silence and just "being."

A few years ago I had a class I believed couldn't be calm and quiet for more than a few minutes. "Too much nervous energy," I told myself. But I was determined to have at least fifteen minutes of silence after lunch each day when the children and I could read or write in our journals. Day by day I introduced them to this practice, starting with only five to ten minutes and gradually extending it. For some of the children, this was the only waking time in their lives that they experienced quiet; and it felt strange initially. But then an interesting thing began to happen. They started loving the silence and actually requesting it for longer periods, having discovered how precious and nurturing silence could be and longing for the feeling of calmness it induced.

Mindfulness

When we are capable of stopping, we begin to see and, if we can see, we understand. Peace and happiness are the fruits of this process. (Thich Naht Hanh, 39)

Beyond silence is *mindfulness*, "an appreciation for the present moment and the cultivation of an intimate relationship with it" (Kabat-Zinn, 5). When we sit in silence, we can experience that moment as the only one that really exists. The past is gone, the future not yet here. The present is all we have. We can honor this particular moment through mindfulness.

How often we do just the opposite! We ignore what's happening in the present, focusing instead on what we have to do next, or what we should have done before. We miss the present moment and its unique essence is lost forever. We are thrust into a swirl of *automaticity*—doing, going, thinking, never mindful of what's happening *right now*.

Author John Kabat-Zinn told us that when we practice mindfulness we gain access to greater wisdom and vitality. In doing so, we improve the direction of our lives and enrich the quality. Emerson, Thoreau, Whitman, and many Native Americans described the essence of mindfulness in their writings. Thoreau, "would often sit in his doorway for hours and just watch, just listen, as the sun moved across the sky and the light and shadows changed imperceptibly . . . times when

[he] could not afford to sacrifice the bloom of the present moment" (35). Appreciating "the bloom of the present moment" is what mindfulness is about.

These days everybody moves so quickly. To what? For what? Is there a valid reason for this frenetic pace, or is it just a manifestation of our automaticity?

"Come on, boys and girls, hurry up and finish your work. Let's go." How often do we say these words to children? I say them far more often than I would like. As aware as I think I am, I still get caught up in life's hectic pace, and I transfer it to my students. Have you noticed how the majority of today's children are on regimented schedules? Many are shifted from one activity to the next when the school day ends: first after-school care; then sports; later, inevitable time before America's most popular electronic babysitter, the TV. What our children learn through this continuous hubub is a dependence on activities outside themselves. Their capacity for silent reverie and autonomous choice-making has been seriously compromised. No wonder so many children show signs of hyperactivity; they have never learned to find a quiet place inside themselves. We need to guide them to that place. But first we must do this for ourselves.

When you get home from work tomorrow try this: Go to a quiet spot; don't turn on the TV or radio; and don't answer the phone if it rings. Just sit and notice the sensations of your body. Breathe deeply and just be in the moment. If thoughts come into your head, let them pass through, but don't focus on any of them. Concentrate instead on your breathing. Look out a window, notice the sky, or close your eyes and listen to the silence. If it's a nice day, do this outside. Quiet your mind and *be in the present moment.*

Try this for ten to fifteen minutes each day, and you'll begin to notice subtle changes. The more mindful you become, the more you will want to stop and just notice things. When you get in your car at the end of the day, don't turn on the radio or start thinking about what you have to do next. Instead just feel the preciousness of the silence, and notice your natural surroundings. Something elemental will be fed; your reverence for life elevated.

Calmness in the Classroom

It's possible also to practice calmness, mindfulness in the classroom. Every day after I've walked my students to the lunchroom, I go back to my room for a few minutes, shut the door, leave the lights off, sit down at my desk and look out the window. I feel the swirl of quelled activity around me, as though the children have left their energy behind. I feel my own exhaustion, or exhilaration, or frustration, depending on what kind of day it's been. I experience the moment as it is before moving onto the next, and in doing so I feel more centered and ready to deal with what lies ahead.

Teach your children to do the same. I have them sit for a moment, breathe deeply and just listen to the silence in the room. Being mindful of the present moment even just briefly can be an invaluable experience for them. I often do this with the children before we begin to write. Often ideas flow more freely as a result.

A variation of this activity is to have each child think of a place that makes her or him feel calm, safe, and happy. I call this their "peaceful place." Some of my students have chosen the ocean, the mountains, their room at home, their grandmother's house, the woods. Next I ask them to sit for a moment and imagine being in that place, breathing deeply as they think. Being mindful of this nurturing place connects the children once again to its calming atmosphere.

When we enable children to experience mindfulness, we give them the gift of a lifelong strategy. If only we all had learned these valuable techniques as children.

Breathing for Calmness

Breathing in, I calm my body. Breathing out, I smile. (Thich Naht Hanh, 10)

During the first week of school I taught Hanh's words to my children. Calmness spread its soft web through our room as we recited them together, breathing and smiling as we did so. This has become one of our favorite daily practices, one which the children ask for when I forget to do it.

Countless times throughout the day we stop and simply breathe together. When the children first enter the room, if I sense an overflow of their nervous energy, I'll say immediately, "OK, everybody, stop what you're doing and let's all take a nice deep breath together." After the first breath, I'll say, "Great, now let's take another one." After that breath I'll say, "Notice how calm the room feels right now? Let's keep that peaceful feeling inside us as we start the day." The children often smile when I say this, knowing how much better they feel when the tenor of the room is calm. This simple activity focuses the children, enabling them to access a calm place within themselves. For children who have ADD or emotional problems, very often, I'll sit or stand close to them and breathe with them several times (or more) throughout the day. This practice of breathing and calming becomes a self-management skill they can take with them into their adult lives.

During transitional times I use breathing to help the children quiet themselves and refocus. For example, if we're ready to move from language arts to math, I might say , "OK, put your papers away and let's all take a deep breath together before we start math." At that point everything stops and I say, "Breathe in and hold it for a moment. Now breathe out." We'll do this several times until we all feel calm and relaxed. In

fact, whenever I feel tension starting to build, I'll pause and say to the children, "Why don't we all take a nice deep breath together." This is a key ingredient in sustaining our peaceful classroom all year long. Be sure to teach the children how to do deep breathing before you introduce any of the above techniques.

Many teachers have found that the simple act of breathing together makes a definable difference in their classrooms. One teacher said, "It's amazing the way the children take to this. It helps them calm down and they know it. Some of my children have asked me to do breathing with them more often throughout the day."

I've told my children to try deep breathing at home when they're nervous, upset, frightened, or angry. "This is something you can do to help yourself feel better under any circumstance. You can go to a quiet place and take a few deep breaths, or you can remain wherever you are and just breathe while you think of your peaceful place." Over the years I have had children tell me they've used breathing for a wide variety of reasons: to help them relax before a test, to alleviate the anxiety they feel if their parents have an argument, to lessen upset feelings and prevent a fight with a sibling, to calm themselves after a bad dream, and many, many more.

Negotiating the path of peacemaking is not an easy task; there are challenges at every turn. Sometimes it seems as though every aspect of our hectic society runs counter to the goal of being peaceful. As in the myth of Sisyphus, our attempts to be peaceful can feel like we're pushing a boulder up a mountain only to have it fall down again and again. Conversely, by weaving into our lives daily practices that bring us calmness amid the tumult, we begin to gain a sense of inner peace that is not contingent upon circumstances. By modeling peacefulness, we help our students to move toward inner peace, thus enabling them to function better in the world.

PART Two

Integrating Writing and Peacemaking

Peacemaking is something very important because if there was no peacemaking people will not be treating others the way they want to be treated and people will be getting hurt all the time. There will be too may wars. . . .

Michael, age 7

CHAPTER Six

Beginning

. . . one of the prime elements of human uniqueness is the ability to create and exercise new options. The ultimate test of education is whether it makes people comfortable in the presence of options: which is to say whether it enables them to pursue their possibilities with confidence.

—Cousins, 17

Beyond learning the skills of peacemaking, there is a need to transform the way people think. Literacy and peacemaking consist not only of skills and methods, they are vehicles for changing the world. Our greatest peacemakers have been highly literate people. Martin Luther King moved millions with his eloquence. Gandhi was highly educated, widely read. Literacy helped to frame their thinking and inspire their vision, thus enabling them to inspire others.

Schools provide skills that can lead to transformation of individuals and the world, and peacemaking is the conduit for transformation. When children learn peacemaking concepts and strategies and write about them in the context of their own lives, they begin to *own* what they have learned. Thus a pedagogical link is formed.

In this chapter you will see how children thrive as peacemakers and writers when the process and content of both areas are interwoven continuously. By creating a safe environment where children accept each other and each other's ideas, the freedom to write is nurtured. Peacemaking and writing become threads of the same fabric. Writing becomes a way of understanding the

peacemaking process as children write to comprehend more fully. The writing process often reveals to us hidden insights, obscured perceptions. As children develop a deeper understanding of peacemaking, they become better able to function in the world at large.

In parts of this chapter I give attention to the writing process, focusing on techniques used to nurture the writing of children with varying abilities. As you read, keep in mind that the nurturing atmosphere of the peaceful classroom is the foundation.

Peacemaking Concepts and the Writing Process

Key concepts of peacemaking cannot be repeated too often in working with children. I weave the following key concepts into all of our discussions, including those about writing.

- Each person is unique, important, and valuable.
- We need to value what each person says, listening astutely so that we can reflect what he or she means to say. In doing so the other person knows whether he or she has been understood.

- Avoid put-downs and negative judgments of another's ideas.
- Show acceptance and respect toward others, especially during our discussions.
- When you disagree, be sensitive to the other person's feelings and respect his or her point of view.

During prewriting activities and revision, these attitudes play a very important role. By cultivating them, we help children have faith in what they have to say and a willingness to voice their ideas. Soon they become more able to take risks in their writing.

Early Writers

Since the first week of school, we started each day with our Peace Pledge followed by writing workshop. Often, we follow the pledge with a discussion of how we demonstrate peacemaking in our daily lives. This kind of duscussion becomes a natural lead-in to writing.

Early in the year I help the children select writing topics on most days, knowing that later they'll find it easier to formulate topics on their own. This morning's discussion and related writing topic are "How I Am A Peacemaker." I'm hoping to see evidence in the children's writing that knowledge of peacemaking is emerging in their actions.

My goals for the children's writing at this time of year are in both the affective and cognitive domains. I strive to build comfort and enjoyment into the process of writing, wanting writing to become a natural form of the children's expression, like speaking, drawing, or block-building. At the same time I work toward building fluency and self-expression by allowing the children to write about things they find important. By teaching peacemaking, teachers create a safe atmosphere that enables writing to thrive. Because acceptance is encouraged and modeled from the first day of school, children are gentler

with each other, and with themselves. This acceptance manifests in a greater freedom to write.

Although the examples in this chapter are of second graders, I believe you will find similarities between these children and those in other grades. You will meet writers of varying abilities who encounter the same struggles that you and I do when we write. Poet Georgia Heard described this struggle in *Writing Toward Home*, where she drew a parallel between writing and the intense fear she felt when lost in a torrential rainstorm in Sabino Canyon. She said, "Sometimes writing feels like I'm lost in the canyon and will lose my way home. Writing is this serious. This much a test of my courage. This scary. Sometimes" (13).

Think of your students for whom writing is this scary. Now imagine the arms of the peaceful classroom enfolding them, soothing their fears, enabling them to have faith in what they have to say. Let's see how this unfolds. Keep in mind as you read the following anecdotes that the peacemaking lessons you read about in Chapter I are being taught simultaneously.

Journal Entry: September 17

For our prewriting discussion I asked the children, "How have you been a peacemaker in your life over the past week? Have you started doing any of the things we've talked about, like helping, caring, being a good listener, or working out conflicts?" Most of the children focus on "caring" and "helping." Kevin talked about being helpful at home and in school. Trying to draw details out of him, I said, "Kevin, tell us what kinds of helpful things you've done at home."

"I helped my mom rake leaves the other day. She was happy."

That would be a good thing to write about," I said. "What about in school," I added, hoping to help him write about a number of details."

"I'm a good listener and I help the people at my table."

"I do that too," said Kristina.

"How do you help, Kristina?" I asked, happy that Kevin's idea has sparked her.

"I give people clues in math and on the playground I help people get off the monkey bars."

"Those ideas would be excellent ones to put into your writing," I commented.

"Boys and girls," I said, "turn to the person you sit across from and tell her or him one way you've been a peacemaker in the past week, either by helping or in another way." I reminded them to take turns sharing ideas, always looking at the person speaking, and asking questions to get more information. Slowly the children began sharing, and before long most of them were fairly animated. While they shared I walked through the room, stopping to talk to those who seemed less involved, hoping to prompt their ideas with my enthusiastic questions and reactions. As I continued to make my way around the room, I also focused attention on children who came up with clear ideas to write about. "Boys and girls," I said after listening to Ben's ideas, "Ben's going to write about how he helps his mom with the dishes and how he went to Hershey Park with his family and offered to give his dad money so he could go on rides." (Lucy Calkins calls this technique "making them famous." This "fame" reinforces the ideas of the child who is focused on while stimulating the thinking of others.)

After about ten minutes of paired sharing, I asked the children to direct their full attention back to me; and I helped them summarize the many ideas they came up with. Now they're ready to begin writing about what they had just discussed. I gave them about ten minutes to do so and asked them to work as quietly as possible so they all could concentrate. As they wrote, I wrote.

Amanda was the first to finish. She came bounding to me, paper in hand, eyes shining, "Look, Mrs. Drew, I already wrote a whole page. Do you want to hear it?!! (I wish I could bottle her enthusiasm and give it to the rest of the class.) Glancing around the room I observed my struggling writers in contrast. Allison was staring into space, her pencil on the table and her foot shaking nervously. She had written three words on her paper and didn't look as though she'd come up with any more, though she had much to contribute during our discussion. "Allison, why don't you write what you said before about working out that conflict with your brother."

"Oh yeah," she said with little enthusiasm. She wrote a sentence and stopped again—stuck. I gently prodded her, unwilling to allow her reticence to hinder the untapped ability I know she possesses. (I try to strike a balance between encouraging my students to strive toward their best, and pushing them too hard.)

Across from Allison sat Terrence, wiggling in his chair and about to fall out of it for the third time. He had written nothing but his name, scrawled across the top of his paper. Writing seemed like the last thing Terrence wanted to do, yet during our prewriting discussion, he was animated and filled with ideas. I gave Terrence a short prompt and affirmed him for the good ideas he had earlier.

I looked over at Ben, who had quickly written three illegible lines and was rushing to finish so that he could begin drawing his picture. Ben' artwork usually consists of people shooting at each other and objects exploding. "Ben, slow down," I said, "You'll have plenty of time to work on your picture. Don't rush. " He wrote another line in the time it took to speak this sentence. "Is this enough?" he asked, looking at me and reaching for the crayons.

"Try to write a little more before you draw, just a little more. What else were you thinking about?" I asked him to prompt more text. "You're smart and have lots of ideas, Ben." 'You just need to put your good ideas on your paper."

Bobby had the lowest portfolio score in language arts, yet he wrote a lot. The problem was that he didn't know what he'd written, and neither did I. As usual, his invented spelling didn't even vaguely resemble the actual words; he didn't use any punctuation; and his capital and lower-case letters were all mixed up. "Bobby, you've written so much already. Read what you have so far," I coaxed him, hoping he'd remember something. He looked down at his paper, struggled to read it, then looked up with a confused expression and said, "I forgot." I asked him to retell me his original ideas, hoping I could find a kernel of them in what now appeared on his paper.

I've noticed that all of these children are verbally expressive; but when they put pencil to paper, the flow of ideas is stemmed. My strategies with them will be to tap their deepest interests as incentives for writing, praise each accomplishment, accept shorter pieces, and have parent volunteers assist them in getting their ideas on paper. An aide will be coming in each afternoon. She can help them with handwriting so that the mechanical aspect of writing won't slow them down so much. Later I'll have them work in pairs. From experience I have found that working together too soon creates dependency. I want each child to know that he or she can write.

Between these two opposite types of writers are a variety of children of varying levels and abilities. Kevin just moved here from a community where writing meant "penmanship." Even though he has an I.Q. of 156, he writes very little, focusing on letter formation and neatness rather than ideas. "Kevin, don't worry about it being so neat, "I whispered, leaning over his shoulder. His eyes looked back at me with an expression of pure disbelief. "In this school, we care more about your ideas than anything else. Just put your thoughts down and don't concentrate so much on how the writing looks." He nodded, as though he couldn't believe what he just heard me say. At this point in the year I want the children to write as freely as possible; therefore, we will not publish their work for a while. First-draft writing is perfectly acceptable at this time, as a means of oiling the creative valves,

enabling the children to think on paper, and lessening their fear of mistakes.

Michael sat next to Kevin. He too came from another school and was obsessed with neatness, letter formation, and correct spelling. "Michael, loosen up," I said. "Remember all those grand ideas you had when we were discussing our topic? Write them down and stop worrying about how they look!" I urged him.

"I don't know how to spell the words," he said.

What word would you like to spell?" I asked "Cousin," he replied. I helped him sound out the word in invented spelling. "See, you could do it all along. You don't need to spell the words in actual spelling for this paper. Invented spelling is fine. Later, when we start publishing our work, we'll concentrate more on spelling. Right now you can spell it the way it sounds," I told him, wondering if I should put that message on a sign. Many of my students are afraid to make mistakes.

I moved to CristiAnne who wrote a little, looked around, got up asked for a drink of water, and then forgot what she was writing. ChristiAnne writes beautifully, but keeping focused is her greatest challenge. "ChristiAnne, do you want to sit in the reading center so that you can concentrate better," I asked her. She's happy to move to this more secluded area, knowing how easily she is distracted by the children around her.

Justin seemed to be very bright and his portfolio scores were high, but he wrote very little. He left three-inch spaces between each word and then stopped writing after a couple of lines. "I'm out of ideas," he said.

"Try rereading what you have and then seeing what new ideas come up," I suggested, "and when you write use your finger like this to help you judge the size of a space." I showed him how to use his finger as a guide.

Christina, Taryn, Matthew, and Hannah wanted me to help them spell every other word. Even though their portfolio assessment indicates that they can read and spell a substantial number of words, when it comes to writing a story, they freeze up, overcome by fear of spelling words wrong. "Boys and girls," I reiterate. It's fine to use invented spelling. **It's your ideas that matter the most.**" Will they ever believe me?

I looked around at the class. Each child, with his or her varying ability, produced something vastly different. I wonder if they'll ever get to a point where ten minutes won't be enough time to write, and all children will have so much to say they won't want to stop. That's what I'm aiming for.

Here are some of the stories the children wrote today on "How I Am a Peacemaker:"

I Help my mom rake levas. And i listen to my Techaer becoase theor mate be something I don't know if I don't listen. I help if thay get into a fite. I help pepale if thay need me.

—by Kevin

I helP My SiSter from My friend because I Like her because sheMy Letter sister be cause I Love her we Play to gier (together).

—by Sara

I help People with their math by giveing them clues. I help people get off the monkey bars. one day my friends Stephanie and Loren got in a fite about hou I like the best I told them I like both of them the samd them they stoped fiting. I like helping others.

—by Kristina

How I m a peacemaker

By helping others am respect other peole olot of time at home and at scool to and be good to them

—by Justin

How I am a eacemaKer I am a PeacemaKer Becas I am Nice I ThinK oTher PeoPle are Nice To.

—by Allison

I halp mom wiaht the daish Whan I go to herse prke I spaned all my monny on daddy. I hallp DaD on games. I Sare. I gote god ose. the And.

—by Ben

[Translation:

I help mom with the dishes. When I go to Hershey Park I spend all my money on daddy. I help Dad on games. I share. I got good notes. The end.]

Reflections on the Children's Early Writing

Looking over these writing samples, I notice that most of my students' discourses on peacemaking relate to "helping others," with the exception of Kristina, who refers to a conflict and its resolution in her story. I make a mental note that in most cases, the children's writing and their perception of what peacemaking is all about are quite rudimentary at this stage of the year.

Observing them today, I'd also noticed how deliberate most of the children were in forming every letter, spelling every word, many of them erasing excessively. I began to wonder if the sparseness of their writing was caused by fear of making mistakes. Lucy Calkins talked about this fear as classic in young writers, saying "A concern for rightness can lead second and third graders to erase so much that they rub holes in their pages" (119). Calkins saw this concern as a healthy step in children of this age, however. She referred to the changes in two children she observed:

Greg and Jenn are only a few months older and a few inches taller than they were near the end of late first grade, but their writing habits have changed markedly. Gone is their easy confidence.

"It is as if the protective coat of egocentricity has been taken away from them," Don Graves has said in describing their new awareness. Jenn and Greg are aware of an audience. With audience awareness comes worry. "Will the kids like

my story? It's messy. It's stupid. It's dumb."
For the first time, they suffer writer's block.

> Ironically, their worries . . . are a sign of
> growth. . . . They look back to assess what
> they have done, and they look forward toward
> an eventual audience. These emerging abilities
> bring new concerns. (118)

Because of many children's self-critical nature, I know that the peaceful, accepting atmosphere will help them become less fearful about writing; but I also know this doesn't happen overnight. Observing writing during these first weeks of school, I can see exactly what Lucy Calkins talked about: Hesitation, and self-doubt clearly shows in the way most of my children approached writing thus far. Also evident is a general lack of understanding about writing elements: plot development, story structure, expanded content, and expression of feelings. Yet I know that the children's writing will take root and grow, aided by the climate of support and acceptance I am working hard to foster, along with a rich literary environment and careful modeling of what makes good writing.

I think of Regie Routman's wise words in *Transitions*: [long quotation]

> Respect allows and promotes choice, trust, and independence. Respect accepts children where they are and encourages and congratulates them for their attempts. Respect values children as unique individuals. The language the teacher uses in talking to children carries the tone of her teaching and lets children know if they are respected. If they feel respected, they will feel secure and be able to take risks. (32)

That is what we need to do for all of our children, and to enable them to do for each other.

When children begin editing, teachers need to be careful that their fragile egos are helped, not hindered, by peer feedback. In modeling, it's important to stress peacemaking as much as writing. In *Schools Without Failure*, William Glasser commented on this subject.

> Once an atmosphere of thinking, discussing, and problem-solving is established, situations that ordinarily cause serious disturbances . . . can be handled effectively within the class. Children learn that their peers care about them. They learn to solve the problems of their world. (131)

How well this idea applies to the process of writing, peer editing, conferencing, and large group discussions.

The Children's Writing Starts to Grow

Literature once again plays a key role. In the following scenario you will see how Dr. Seuss's *The Butter Battle Book* is used for the dual purpose of teaching peacemaking and writing. This powerful book tells of a war between the Yooks and the Zooks. The Yooks eat their bread with the butter side up; the Zooks, with the butter side down. Dr. Seuss carefully weaves into the story the issues of prejudice, stereotyping, otherness, escalation of conflict, use of weapons, and the roots of war. After reading *The Butter Battle Book*, we had one of our most involved discussions, which revealed to me that the children already have been influenced by lessons in peacemaking.

Journal Entry: October 3

"Why did the gray people (the Yooks) have to make all those weapons just 'cause the other people ate their bread on the butter side down?" asked Matthew.

I think they should've talked about it instead of making weapons. Weapons are bad. You can kill people with them," added Kevin.

If the guy dropped his bomb, then everyone could die, even his own people; what good would that do?" said Caitlin.

"I think the guy didn't like the other people because they were brown." said Arjay. (I wondered if Arjay said this because his own skin is brown.)

"I think everyone should learn peacemaking. Then there won't be any more wars." added Amanda.

"That's my hope," I said.

At this point Ben, a great proponent of war, weapons, and fighting, raised his hand with a sense of urgency. He had been deep in thought during the discussion, and looked as though he had come to some kind of realization. "It's not good to fight," he said as though grasping this idea for the first time. "People should talk it out instead. They should use I messages."

I smiled inside and out as I digested what Ben had just said and quickly reinforced his idea to the class: "What Ben's talking about, when people work out differences using words instead of using their fists or weapons, is called "negotiations," and that's exactly what the President is doing in Washington today." (It's Day 2 of the Mideast Peace Summit.) "It's the same thing we're learning about in school, talking out differences. Ben, you're absolutely right. That **is** a better thing to do."

Ben's comment and my response to it opened up another facet of discussion, and the children started talking about events in the news: shootings, murders, kidnappings, child abuse, bombings. They were aware beyond their years of such happenings, too aware. Joanna Macy, in *Despair and Personal Power in the Nuclear Age,* stated that talking about our fears is the first step toward moving beyond them. She posited that providing steps they can take in their personal lives can help people feel less powerless. I have seen this happen with children. When they feel they have control over some the events in their daily lives, they feel less frightened about events outside of themselves. Hence, when they have a strategy for working out their own conflicts, they feel empowered and can

generalize this feeling to the larger world. An ongoing integrated discourse about peacemaking serves this purpose for many children.

When the children came in this morning, they asked to write about solutions they had come up with to solve the Butter Battle. (The author left the book open ended). What had now become 20 minutes of silent writing time stretched even longer today. The children didn't want to stop writing. "Can we have some more time?" asked Matthew. "I have a lot more I want to write about." So many voices chimed in that I decided to put our usual schedule on hold and just let the children write as long as they needed. For some a half hour was enough. For others it was not. "I want to take this home and work on it some more," said Kristina. "I want to make it into a book." Great idea, Kristina," I said. Many of the children have started making books. They choose their best works, revise and then publish them. Three more hands shot up asking to do the same. It occurred to me that we were moving toward the goal I had set on the first day of school: the children have become so absorbed in writing that they're asking for more time. It was really happening! Even Ben and Terrence were completely engaged.

When I looked at the finished product of today's writing, I noticed an overall improvement. My strong writers have gotten stronger, extending their stories, editing more carefully, revising, using more colorful language and even incorporating some dialogue. My average writers are becoming more comfortable expressing themselves, spelling their own words, taking risks, and editing more independently than before. My weakest writers are actually writing now. They may not write a lot, but what they write, they do with feeling, enjoyment, and a greater degree of independence. Bobby can now read some of his own stories, and I'm able to decipher a lot of his words as well. Terrence has surprised me by becoming quite absorbed in his stories. Once he focuses, he can produce some fairly cohesive pieces. And Allison's latent creativity is starting to surface. Sometimes she even incorporates rhymes and poems into her writing. Christina has become less dependent on others to prompt ideas and help her spell; today's story was one of her best. Kevin and Michael have begun to loosen up. Today they each wrote one of his longest stories thus far. Kelsey, one of my top writers, is writing insightful, animated pieces. Look at some of their work:

Here's How I'd Help Solve the Butter Battle
I wold say, "stop. we bothe can get cilled if he dropped it. I wold get him on my back and run. I wold say, "Pleys dont fite because I dont want to die and you dont want to die."

—by Terrence

I woold help by talking It out and maybe they will be friend's. I would say to them, "It will taste the saem. you and you are juste fithing over something sille." I woold make them say to ech oather, "I prameis we will not have a nother waer."

—by Christina C.

I would say, "stop"! but if they don't and drop the bomb I will try to cach the bomb and then I wad talk it out. By telling them "why are you fighting over something silly? And I would tell them to destroy the weapons. Stop fighting over something silly and now that I told you what to do keep doing it.

—by Kevin

Here's how I'd help them solve the Butter Battle. To StoP the Butter Battle Here'S What I Wiuld. I Would saY "don't droP The bomb or You'll boeTh die. So don't Think about it. Don't even try.

—by Allison

I would say, "don't fight, talk it out." I would have them apullagise. They would say "I'm sorry." I think thy shouldent use weapons. I think they should use words. think it is silly

what they foght about. I would say "we're different on the outside but we're all the same inside. I say you should shake hands. I think you shoud be friends. There's no wrong way to eat butter on bread. In the future I would make shore there wouldent be any weapons. And they wouldent droop the boomb. I would also tell them to use I messages.

—by Kelsey

Reflections

This lesson provided a valuable scaffold for both story development and the ability to imagine alternatives. The basic message was that if we are to change our own behaviors, we must first be able to see new possibilities; if we aspire to transform the world in which we live, we must start with a vision of what it can be. Concurrently, when we attempt to write about any of these concepts, we must first imagine alternatives. I modeled all of this in our prewriting activities and in the discussion after reading *The Butter Battle Book*. The writing that emerged was far richer than anything the children had written before. Their discourse on peacemaking now includes the following concepts:

- We must talk out our differences rather than fighting.
- War is futile.
- No conflict is worth dying for.
- Large conflicts can be ignited by foolish issues.

Kelsey's piece had a marvelous complexity, incorporating such phrases as:

- "Don't fight, talk it out."
- "We're different on the outsied but we're all the same on the inside."
- "I would tell them to use I messages."

Kevin's writing, like Kelsey's, has a sophistication beyond many of his peers. Both children demonstrate an ability to conceive new realities through their writing, each incorporating dramatizations of dialogue, hypothetical reasoning, and imagined outcomes.

In *Social Worlds of Children Learning to Write*, Anne Haas Dyson wrote, ". . . through the construction of symbolic worlds . . . relationships between people can be reconceived and transformed." Through reading, writing, role play, puppetry and discussion, the children in my class have begun to reconceive their worlds. *The Butter Battle Book* enabled them to look at some of their deepest fears and see beyond them. The children began to look at solutions to the problems of war, conflict, and prejudice. The continuous infusion of peacemaking skills into the daily curriculum is helping the children see options not only for themselves but for others. I think of Norman Cousins' words: "...one of the prime elements of human uniqueness is the ability to create and exercise new options. The ultimate test of education is whether it makes people comfortable in the presence of options: which is to say whether it enables them to pursue their possibilities with confidence" (17). Cousins is not just talking about options on a personal level. Much to the contrary, he believes that peace starts with each individual and that through individuals exercising positive options, we can begin reshaping the future—the primary role of education.

How does this belief relate to writing? Today's writing was a prime example of what Peter Elbow talked about in *Writing With Power:* ". . . a topic of personal importance and an urgent occasion" can enable people of even marginal writing abilities to become good writers. (7) I posit that this is what's happened with Terrence and Allison, and suspect that their absorption in this topic pushed them beyond themselves in spite of fine motor difficulties, attentional problems, and past failures.

By engaging my students in the kind of hypothetical reasoning that went on today, their thinking and writing moved into a larger context. The juxtaposition of writing skills and social skills enabled the children to look beyond individual concerns, examine crucial issues people care about collectively, and then integrate these issues in their stories. My students are beginning to stretch as thinkers, as writers, and as human beings.

The Teacher's Role in Children's Growth

A favorite graduate school professor of mine constantly encouraged me to scrutinize my actions with students to identify what made my teaching successful. She would have me dissect the dynamics of my teaching as a detective dissects a case, looking for clues to "what made things work." As I reflected upon the preceding journal entry and asked myself, "What made things work for me?" I came up with a variety of responses.

- *My enthusiasm for writing.* It spilled over to the children almost immediately. What teacher hasn't had the experience of sharing passions with students, and having the students become passionate about the same things. When we teach what we love, we teach from a source of inspiration; and inspiration is infectious.
- *Refusal to accept any child's history as a limitation.* Each child comes into my classroom with a clean slate. I teach to their strengths, not their weaknesses, expecting the best from all of them and not settling for less.
- *A combination of firmness and fairness.* My students know I love them, but I don't take any nonsense. When it's time to write, it's time to write. Our writing workshop is a sacred part of the day—as is all learning—and I expect students to regard it as such. I regard school as the place where the world's most important work goes on, and my students know this. They respond accordingly.
- *Continuous reinforcement of even the smallest steps toward progress.* "Ryan, you wrote four lines today, that's great! Yesterday you wrote

only three lines. You're improving and I'm proud of you." Statements like this constantly bolster my students' self-esteem and enthusiasm. They feel good about what they're doing, even if they never have before; and they begin to focus on their own successes. This success makes them want to do more.

• *Sharing my own process with them.* "Boys and girls," I say, holding up the scribbled pages of my journal," I'm working on a poem; and I can't get it right. Look, I've done five drafts and I still don't have it the way I want it. But I'm not giving up. Maybe the next draft will be just right." One of the best experiences my students was when I brought in a chapter of this book, returned from an editor. When I showed them all the red marks and changes the editor had made, they squealed with delight. One of them said, "Mrs. Drew, you make more mistakes than we do!" From this simple, but valuable lesson the children saw that writing doesn't have to be perfect, that grown-ups make mistakes, and that the process of writing involves risk for people of all ages.

CHAPTER Seven

Continued Growth

The thing above all, that a teacher should endeavor to produce in . . . pupils if democracy is to survive is the kind of tolerance that springs from an endeavor to understand those who are different from ourselves.

—Bertrand Russell, qtd. in Knowles, 529

Integrating Diversity, Writing, and Peacemaking

Journal Entry: November 4

Since school started I've been weaving the issue of diversity into our class discussions. I have read the children a wide variety of stories that touch on diversity in its many forms; we've listened to related songs; and we've read pertinent poetry. This month our community has been the host of an exhibition about Anne Frank, which many of my students' parents have attended. Although my students are too young to attend the exhibition themselves, many of them now know the story of Anne Frank through their parents. Today one of the children said, "Did you know that Anne Frank had to live in an attic and these bad people were trying to kill her and her family?" Before I had a chance to answer, many of the other children began to raise questions about Anne Frank. I decided to tell the whole class her story.

Afterwards I wrote the words "discrimination" and "prejudice" on the board, asking if anyone remembered what these words meant. I had introduced them in September during a discussion

about Martin Luther King, Jr. Several children remembered and one them said, "Discrimination is when people are mean to other people because they're different on the outside." A heated discussion ensued, and the children talked about incidences of prejudice or discrimination they were aware of. Terrence, who's African-American said, "I saw this movie and there were people in it who dressed up like ghosts and they wanted to hurt the black people." I told the children about the Ku Klux Klan, and drew a comparison between the behavior of the Klan and the Nazis. As young as my students are, none of this information was new to them. I was pleased they had an awareness, but troubled that we live in a world where seven year-olds need to be cognizant of such harsh truths.

I decided to use this opportunity to draw a parallel to their own lives. "Have you ever heard anyone make fun of another person because of the color of that person's skin? or religion? or handicap? or because he is a boy or she is a girl?" Several children related stories about different forms of prejudice, but, interestingly, none was personal. I wondered if these children had never been victims of prejudice, or were they perhaps too uncomfortable to talk about personal situations? Finally Amanda raised her hand and said, almost tearfully, "I was made fun of for being a girl. I was trying to climb up to the top of the monkey bars and this boy kept saying, 'Get down, you can't do it. You're just a girl'."

"How did that make you feel, Amanda?" I asked.

"Real bad, really bad. It kind of made me feel like I just couldn't do it," she said, looking down at the floor.

"Amanda, how brave of you to share that story," I responded. "I hope you know that you really **can** do almost anything you set out to do. Girls are just as able as boys." Amanda looked up and smiled.

"Boys and girls, what Amanda just described is a form of prejudice too. I'm wondering if you know what to do if you're ever in a situation like that."

"Tell somebody?" one of the children ventured.

"Yes," I answered, "or say something directly to the person who made the remark, an I message, like, 'I don't want to be spoken to that way. It's disrespectful."

Amanda said, "I couldn't say anything. I was too upset."

"I can see why," I said, "That remark would have been upsetting. You know, boys and girls, if you're ever with anyone in Amanda's situation, you can say something too."

"Like, 'I don't want you talking to my friend that way. It's not right,'" said Taryn.

"Alissa did that on the playground. She stuck up for her friend when this kid said something mean," Taryn added.

"That's a brave thing to do, and that's something I hope you'll all try if you're ever in a similar situation."

"It's hard to say that kind of thing," said Hannah.

"It **is** hard, " I agreed, "but we all need to speak up because that can stop people from mak-

ing put-downs about people who are different. It's the same with jokes. If someone makes a joke that puts down people because of their color, religion or anything else, say something. It's the only way to stop it. People have to speak up. That's what peacemaking is about."

After that discussion, we wrote. Here are Justin and Terrence's stories.

> There was a movie called Best of the Best 3, no tuning back. There was man that was black. But he get kiled because they put a base ball on his hede an got a bat, and hit the ball off. it wold be like a nut krcked. his hed got krcked. A little boy was criing.
>
> —by Terrence

> Anne Frank died in wrold war two. she hied in the attic for a long time but one day they fond her and she was sent to a camp called a consentreson camp and she got keled in the camp. so a bad president came but one day he shot him self and every body was happy agen. I feel bad that Anne Frank died because she was a human bean and she was a nice person.
>
> —by Justin

Reflections

This activity enabled the children to engage in a discourse on prejudice, discrimination, and even genocide, through specific examples. After defining and explaining each term, the children were asked to look at their own experiences to see if they could uncover personal examples of such. We then moved back and forth between ideas and examples. This technique is the same technique used in writing; by having it modeled orally, the children were then prepared to include abstract concepts in their stories, moving back and forth between ideas and examples as they wrote. This process challenged the children to make their knowledge significant and to access deeper meanings.

Although Terrence's writing is still at a very rudimentary stage in contrast with many other children in the class, including Justin, he brings to it a depth of feeling, and often shows a high degree of perceptiveness. His use of simile, "it would be like a nut krcked" and even intertextuality as he reexamined a movie, this time with an awareness of prejudice and its ramifications, shows a sophistication not yet evident in the work of many of his peers.

In some ways I found Terrence's story to be more sophisticated than Justin's, even though Justin's piece had a lot more sequenced detail. Justin found himself deeply engaged in a personal discourse about prejudice as he questioned why Anne Frank, "a nice person and human being," should be forced to die. Yet he interjects an almost-fairy tale quality when he says (of Hitler), "a bad president came but one day he shot him self and everybody was happy agen." I look at this in contrast to Terrence's poignant ending, "his hed got krcked. A little boy was criing."

As I reflect on these pieces and others like them, what becomes clearly validated to me is the importance of having our children engage in a dialogue about ethical dilemmas such as these, and to assign writing topics from time to time that will force them to grapple with moral issues. Prejudice, discrimination, all forms of racism are too crucial to be ignored. We can't leave these topics to chance, allowing them to be random offshoots of classroom discussions. We need to have a structure for teaching about crucial issues, at the same time connecting them to the writing process. In doing so we provide another means for children to confront the issues of prejudice and discrimination and their concomitant outcomes, in hopes that discourse will someday give rise to solutions.

Growth in the Affective and Cognitive Domains

As teachers our goal is greater than just passing on facts and information. If we want our students to be caring human beings, then we need to respond to them in caring ways. If we value our children's dignity, then we need to model the methods that affirm their dignity. (Faber and Mazlish , 42)

You will notice that peacemaking takes hold at different rates with different classes. The longer you teach peacemaking the sooner it will take hold in each new class, and the more you reinforce, the quicker the progress with any group. During the two years I observed my classes in preparation for the writing of this book I was absolutely diligent about reinforcing peacemaking every day. I looked for opportunities to affirm positive behaviors, read peacemaking related literature to the children several times a week, showcased the Win/Win Guidelines, reviewed our Peaceful Classroom chart, followed our Peace Pledge with a discussion almost every morning, and integrated peacemaking skills into other areas of the curriculum. Because of this continuous effort, a cohesive peaceful classroom came together by the beginning of November, perhaps earlier than some teachers experience. Diligence, I am convinced, was the key.

Journal Entry: November 13

Looking around this classroom , I can say, "yes, it's happening." I have a truly peaceful classroom now. Something intangible has occurred, like a ray of light coming on the horizon, without my noticing. Things have started to change; though it doesn't always happen this quickly. Lately I've noticed that a certain gentleness pervades the room. Acknowledgements of personal responsibility, a willingness to resolve conflicts, the ability to do so independently, and a lessening of conflicts— all that is, indeed, happening.

Today I sat back and observed my students writing in small groups, helping each other spell and edit. As they conferred with each other, I heard them offering support, giving each other compliments, listening intently to one another's thoughts. And I said again, yes, peacemaking has taken hold. The children no longer depend on me to own this process. They own it.

Ben is a changed person. Despite serious attention problems, he has stopped fighting, reflects on his actions, and has found a new place for himself. The same child who stalked the halls last year, now offers people help and hugs his teacher often. He may be the staunchest proponent of peacemaking this school has.

Terrence has also grown a lot since September. He's still impulsive, but he thinks more before reacting and shows more sensitivity toward his peers. The other day he happily announced to the class, "I'm a peacemaker now. I stop fights with my brother before they even start, and I don't kick anyone when I play soccer anymore. It feels good."

Justin has developed a greater conscience. "Yesterday I did something different," he said at sharing time. "I was at my friend's house and I broke his building by mistake, but instead of lying like I usually did I was honest about it. I told him what I did and then I offered to help him build another building."

Allison proudly told the class what she and her friends have been doing out on the playground: "My friends and I helped people prevent conflicts. We walked around and if we saw a problem we said something. Like this girl was going the wrong way on the slide. We talked to her."

Taryn has had some serious problems getting along with her sister. She came in the other day and shared how proud she was for compromising: "My sister needed something I had, and I just gave it to her without complaining. I felt good about that."

Each day the children have had an opportunity to share ways they've been peacemakers, and struggles they have had along the way . It's never a straight and even road. We talk about our challenges (including my own) openly and honestly, and we problem-solve together. A sense of camaraderie and shared mission has come out of this, and I am inspired by the changes I see. The children are learning to honor the complexity of conflicts and resolutions in life. This, in turn enables them to do the same in their writing as they honor the process of integrating new ideas, finding new solutions.

Concurrent Growth in Writing

As peacemaking continues to permeate the lives and thoughts of my children, their writing grows in leaps and bounds. As already noted, one process reinforces the other.

Recently I wrote the following words on the board:

content
flow
detail
transitions
leads
endings

We talked about the meaning of each word as we shared our written stories. The children gave feedback to the writers whose stories they shared, using these words as a framework. I helped them analyze the strengths and weaknesses of their writing, noticing that the majority found this to be nonthreatening within the safe, nurturing atmosphere of our peaceful classroom. For example, after Caitlin read her story aloud, Taryn said, "I liked your story. It had a good lead, but I thought you could have said a little more at the end."

I reread Caitlin's lead aloud to illustrate its strength: "I think peacemaking's important. It is important because it makes your life better."

"Notice how Caitlin's lead draws you into the story and makes you want to read on," I said. "What else would you like to know about at the end?" I asked.

"I'm not sure," said Taryn. Maybe Caitlin could just say something else about being a peacemaker."

"I kind of like it the way it is," said Caitlin. Amanda read her story next.

Why I Am a Peacemaker
by Amanda

I am a peacemaker because I help people when they are hurt. I try to help people solve their problems. Onse I got in a fight with one of my best friends Allson because I told Crissy that I didn't like when Allison was always bracin prommis on me. Then Chrissy told a sixth-grader. The sixth grader told Allson, which me, Allison and Chrissy got upset. Then we all gave each other an I Message and we were friends. Are You A Peacemaker?

Justin commented on its nice flow and ending but said he was wondering about the part with the sixth-grader. I concurred and asked Amanda if there were some way she could expand on that part some more to make it a little clearer. "Yeah, said Terrence, "How about a little more detail." Amanda digested our comments and nodded.

"Sometimes when we conference about our writing we find parts we want to change. Other people's questions and feedback can really help us improve our work," I commented. "When you listen to someone else's story and ask them to tell you more about the parts that are not clear to you, you're helping them expand their thinking and writing."

More and more, the children incorporated writing process terminology as they offered insightful questions and comments, all the while taking care to be gentle with each other's feelings.

- "Great story, but I think it needs more of an ending. Can you tell us more about what happened that day?"
- "Your content was good, but you need a lead at the beginning."
- "Your story had a good flow. It made me want to listen."

I don't want the children to be afraid of revision or to believe they're not good writers if they have to revise. I told them how hard adult writers work at getting things just right, and how we also revise based on the feedback of others. Many times I've shown them scribbled revisions in my journals and other writings, encouraging them not to be afraid to cross out and change things. "Look," I said, showing them a piece I had revised several times and still hadn't finished, "I crossed out so much I can hardly see what I've written. It's a mess!" They giggled and agreed with me. "But my revisions are making this better," I added, hoping they would follow my lead. Revision is so difficult for children. They treasure their words and don't want to make many changes. But isn't revision of writing like revision of life, a form of change? Change is scary. As peacemakers we must "re-vision" ourselves and our world, imagining new possibilities, just like we do when we revise our writing.

Today's writing followed, once again, a discussion about peacemaking. The following stories are the results. As I read them, I was impressed not only with the content but also with the sensitivity so many of my students have begun to exhibit. Take a look.

Why Peacemaking Is Important
by Kristina

Peacemaking is important in lots of ways, like helping other people, caring about other people.

People like my friends get in lots of fights. I try to get them to com down so they can say their sorry. If there were no peacemaking in the world there would be lots of wars because know one would no peacemaking.

Last year my friend found me at home playing in my backyard and she said, "come to my house!" I was with my mom and my dad and she pulled me out of my backyard to her house. When my parents came out to see what I was doin they couldn't find me in my backyard so they looked for me at my friend's house. They found me there and my friend got me in trubble. The next day I gave my friend a stricked

I message on the bus. She didn't say it back so I told the bus driver. He put my friend in the front of the bus. The bus driver made my friend say the I message back to me. Then we were friends again.

I have changed now that I know peacemaking. When I was five and my brother was almost four I used to fuss a lot with him. When I got home from school he always had a friend over and I had to do my homework so i never got to go to one of my friends houses. Sometimes I still fuss with my brother because he still doesn't have any homework. Evry day I try to give him a I message but he doesn't know them yet. I'm going to help him learn to give I messages. Peacemaking is really important so learn it!

Notice how Kristina tells a multi-layered story touching on global as well as personal peacemaking. Kristina's theme reflects her struggle to be a peacemaker in the face of inner and outer conflict. The tension between herself and her little brother is a very real part of her life, yet she seeks within herself an altruistic place; from this vantage point she recognizes her desire to talk out conflicts and notes how difficult this is. In the classroom as well, when Kristina casts herself in the role of peacemaker, she feels better inside, and sees that she can rise above the conflicts that otherwise tend to ensnare her.

Kevin's story (below) also reveals a discourse that mingles global as well as personal themes. He is aware of the violence in our world and sees himself as someone who takes responsibility, teaching others peacemaking, and helping at home. Kevin sees the connection between individual and collective acts.

Why Peacemaking Is Important

by Kevin

Peacemaking is Important because if knowbody knows about it everybody would be fighting. Peacemaking is fun but if everybody knows about peacemaking it would be the aposit.

everybody would live in peace. Somebody mite get hert too and not many people know about peacemaking and a lot of people get hert or kiled and it's up to us to teach everybody peacemaking. A lot of people try to hert or kill people and if they do we have to put them in jail and we don't want to do that, so teach everybody peacemaking. and this is something I did to be a peacemaker. I help around the house and help clean my brothers mass. I help clean some places. The point is teach everybody peacemaking.

In contrast to Kevin's and Kristina's pieces, Terrence's writing, while showing a growing perceptiveness, still reflects a discourse relating more to his smaller world than to the larger. He has begun to re-envision himself as a peacemaker, however. Today's story demonstrates an awareness of cause and effect, clearly indicating the progress he has made both in writing and in peacemaking.

How Peacemaking Helps Me

by Terrence

Peacemaking is fun. When you treet others the wey you want to be treeted. And they will treet you right. a Peacemaker is someone who teels the trooth. Who dose not fight, or dus not shuv. So don't you worry because they won't fight you. I do peacemaking to. I never let my brother down. I play with him. My brother left for Callafonya.

Like Terrence, Ben is extremely immature and this immaturity clearly manifests in his writing. He, too, has begun constructing a new image of himself. Ben now takes great pride in the care he shows for others and the efforts he makes to get along with his peers. He talks about this frequently, hoping that others too have noticed the changes he's made. Ben's story lacks a plot, though, and shows no conflict to be resolved. It is basically a list of things he does to be a peacemaker, which, nevertheless, denotes the significant progress he has made both in writing and social skills. For him writing has become a tool through which he can continue to re-imagine himself.

How Peacemaking Changed My Life
by Ben

Hi I am Ben. I'm going to tall you why peacemaking is good. I know peacemaking becase I learn at scool. When I get to scool I share. After I share I play vidyo Games. and I hlap Ricke beat the Bad guy. When I get to scool and out side for resas I kick the Ball for Kevin. and I swing the tier swing and I kick the flip Ball for my fierds and I gave the tikit out foR Terrence. and I werk out Conflicts. I tret pepol what they wont to Be treted and I geve pepol what thy wont.

I treat people the Way they want to Be treated. I give people eye messages.

Caitlin; Justin; and Amanda, whose story appears several pages back, are more mature writers, although their stories do not reflect a world view of peacemaking as did Kevin's and Kristina's. They see peacemaking on a personal level, writing about how important it is to use the skills with their friends. Their stories are rich and complex in a different way.

Why Peacemaking Is Important
by Caitlin

I think peacemaking is Important. It is Important because it makes your life better. It makes your conflicts turn out so much better. You need to be a peacemaker. If you don't know peacemaking you won't be good at conflicts. Mrs. Drew told us all about peacemaking. Mrs. Drew tells us to treat others with respect. Mrs. Drew told us to live by the Golden Rule. I Love peacemaking.

I had a conflict once. My friend Kelsey was in it. I said to Kelsey that her overals were bad. I said I was sorry. Kelsey said it was ok. We became friends gain. I said I did not like your overals. I think I said it becuse I was Jalis. I think necks time I should just say nothing.

A Conflict I Resolved
by Justin

At my friends house Drew had a conflict with Ben and they waer verey mad and I stoped it from sprading. So I whent over to them and said "Why don't you give him an I message instead of telling on Ben." So Drew gaive him an I message and they waer friends agen. And they never fighted agen.

Why peacemaking is important. Peacemaking is verey important. why? Because it's verey helpful. Another thing about peacemaking it's a verey good thing to do. In my life and in evrybody in this class cares about peacemaking. Exspesley me.

I helped in 1st grade with the affter school program.. With games and crafts and with helpeng the teacher. In the class room. That's how I'm a peacemaking boy in this school.

Michael's story, below, turned out to be one of the most interesting to me. Michael is not one of the more mature children in the class, nor is he one of the better writers, yet his story was as multi-layered, complex, and broad in scope as Kevin's and Kristina's. He sees the connection between peacemaking and the prevention of war, as well as the need to take personal responsibility for one's actions. He cites examples, moving back and forth between abstract concepts and real-life situations.

Why Peacemaking Is Important
by Michael

I am a peacemaker by helping others. Peacemaking is something very important becose if there was no peacemaking people will not be treting others the whay they whant to be tretid and people will be geting hert all the times. there will be to meny wors and hondrids of people get kiled in wors. befor there was lots of wors. My granpa fot in a wor befor. and he is stel living. people are yousing peacemaking now. I think peacmaking is very in portin to evryboty aspeshle this hol class.

We are gust starting to lern peacmaking and we are doing a lot. we red are peas pleg. we sad live by the goldin rull. The goldin rull is very in portin.

Reflections

These stories reflect the moral development of the children who wrote them. Caitlin's story, for example, shows evidence of conscience; she attributes a motive to her negative actions toward Kelsey: "I said I did not like your overalls. I think I said it becuse I was jealous." Kristina struggles over an ongoing conflict with her brother, and looks inside herself for answers: "I still fuss with my brother because he still doesn't have any homework. Every day I try to give him an 'I message,' but he doesn't know them yet. I am going to help him learn to give 'I messages.'" She is no longer willing to continue fighting with her brother. She anticipates that the same skills that have helped her get along with peers in school can help at home.

The children have begun to see that actions have consequences, not only on a personal level, but on a global scale as well. Michael realizes that the most extreme level of conflict is war, and that if people don't practice peacemaking "there will be too many wars and hundreds of people get killed in wars." He, like many of his classmates, is beginning to have an internal dialogue and to imagine its external ramifications. They have moved toward more complex moral and intellectual reasoning as they think and write about motives, explanations, outcomes, and solutions.

John Dewey told teachers that the social environment we create in the classroom is crucial not only to a child's development but to the propagation of the democracy. In his early book, *Democracy and Education* he wrote, ". . . social environment forms the mental and emotional disposition of behavior in individual . . ." Recalling the Johnson and Johnson research cited in Chapter 1, I am beginning to see connections. The social and intellectual environment created through the infusion of peacemaking into the curriculum has enabled the children to learn, interact, and write in an atmosphere of trust and safety.

I'm seeing results in the affective and cognitive domains. As my students are readying to leave the level of concrete operations (ages 2 to 7), defined by Piaget, their representations are taking on a more mature form. They are drawing less, writing more, and doing so with greater depth, meaning, and complexity. Moral reasoning is infused into their writing and thinking now.

Piaget said: "A key period in the continuous development of affective autonomy is during the concrete operational stage when children morally move from a view of moral reasoning based on a unilateral respect to a view based on mutual respect. Cooperative social relations . . . when children are respected and treated as equals are necessary." I'm seeing how developmentally appropriate it is to be weaving peacemaking into the curriculum, particularly at this stage of students' lives. Perhaps they take to peacemaking enthusiastically because it meets a need in their emerging moral development. Ben and Terrence are prime examples. I feel as though peacemaking is filling a well in them that might otherwise be empty, and I'm very happy to have stumbled along this path thirteen years ago.

When Children Bring Up Delicate Issues

You will notice that when children are in an atmosphere of acceptance, safety, and trust, many will open up very comfortably, sometimes too comfortably for a public setting. Issues of divorce, alcohol, or drug abuse, and family squabbles are some of the many topics that could come up. I've had this happen many times over the years, and you may experience the same as peace begins to permeate your classroom. Here's what you can do should a delicate situation arise.

- If a child starts talking about a personal situation in front of the class, tell the child you'd like to discuss it with him or her privately later. Tell the class that if they have personal issues on their minds they can always bring them to you privately, but some problems are meant to be kept confidential. Explain the meaning of confidentiality.
- Speak to the child and find out what's going on, then immediately bring the problem to your principal, guidance counselor, or nurse. As children's home lives become increasingly disrupted, teachers are often put into the role of counselor, one for which we have not been trained and cannot be expected to take on. Don't try to give advice for situations beyond the boundaries of school. Allow the child to tell you what the problem is. Then promptly bring the problem to a professional within your building who has been approriately trained to handle it.

CHAPTER Eight

Validation Through Research

While writing this book I have grappled with the question, "How can I show the relevance of peacemaking to writing?" I have always known that by creating a peaceful classroom I enable my children to learn and socialize in an atmosphere of calmness, acceptance and respect. I do not question that the classroom environment affects cognition, positively or negatively. Also, the process of peacemaking with its related problem-solving, envisioning, and discussions of cause and effect, has taught skills the children could then apply to writing. But beyond that, I wondered if there was another tie-in.

An answer began to emerge as I continued reading extensively about cognitive and intellectual development. Piaget wrote:

> Representation and particularly spoken language are instrumental in the development of social feelings. Representation allows for the creation of images of experiences, including affective experiences. Thus . . . feelings can be represented and recalled. In this way, affective experiences come to have an effect that can last longer than the experiences themselves. (qtd. in Wadsworth, 77)

Representing experiences and feelings through writing enables children to extend the life of each experience and feeling. Piaget explained that representation has that capacity.

In pondering Piaget's ideas, I think I've found what I've been looking for: the relevance of representation and its ability to extend the "shelf life" of ideas. Written expression has the capacity to do this; hence, by writing about ideas, strategies, outcomes, insights, and literature relating to peacemaking, children are prolonging the relevance of each. "I think, therefore I am." I write, therefore I remember. Can that be so? Does representation have such power?

I searched Piaget's writings. In an article titled "Intelligence and Affectivity: Their Relationship During Child Development," I found it again. In this article Piaget said:

> Representation and language allow feelings to acquire a stability and duration they have not had before. Affects, by being represented, last beyond the presence of the object that excites them. This ability to conserve feelings makes interpersonal and moral feelings possible. (44)

When my children write about moral issues such as prejudice, discrimination, racism, and sexism, their feelings and understandings about these issues live longer than when they merely thought about these topics. They've begun to think in more complex ways, going back and forth between examples and concepts, assigning motives to actions, analyzing behaviors, moving their minds out of the microcosm of the personal and into the macrocosm of the larger world. All of this manifests itself in their writing, and if Piaget is right, these thoughts now have "a stability and duration they have not had before."

Writing is an integral part of my classroom. A day doesn't go by that the children don't write (and I write along with them). We write not only to hone the craft of writing; we write to understand our worlds better, and to understand ourselves. Writing is a lens through which questions formulate and clarify, insights reveal themselves, and experiences become validated. Justin's secondhand experience of the Anne Frank exhibition, first seen through his mother's eyes, became clearer and more real through our class discussion; then, further validated through his written story.

Caitlin's desire to understand her conflict with Kelsey eventually lead to the realization in writing that jealousy might have been at the core of her behavior. This is all part of the progression Piaget refers to. Inner life takes on an outer persona when we give words to thoughts. We then honor our words further by putting them into print. Other people's verbalizations give us new pause for thought, and a certain synergy occurs. The spoken word and the written word give birth to new thoughts, and the cycle continues in a triangular schema.

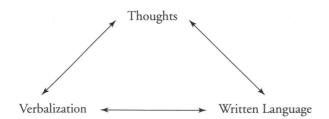

This is the progression that gives our ideas and experiences deeper meaning. Is this another reason my children have developed a love of writing—because it further validates their experiences and ideas? All of a sudden, a thought becomes a poem, journal entry, or story. Thoughts enter the temporal realm, a concrete dimension.

Let me take this reasoning a step further. Paulo Freire in *Pedagogy of the Oppressed* spoke about the significance of true dialogue. He believed that our words have the power to change the world.

> ". . . true dialogue cannot exist unless the dialoguers engage in critical thinking - thinking which discerns an indivisible solidarity between the world and the people . . . thinking which perceives reality as process, as transformation, rather than as a static entity - thinking which does not separate itself from action. . . . (73)

When children learn peacemaking they are, in essence, learning that they have value in this world, and that their actions make an impact on others and upon the world itself. Ben reimages himself, thinking and writing his way into a new persona. Kristina re-evaluates her past behavior patterns and looks for new options. Children are suddenly aware of cause and effect relationships, realizing that when one chooses to act in a violent or divisive manner, one then leaves a negative imprint on one's environment. Conversely, children begin to see that their words, actions, and attitudes can affirm the dignity of others, helping to build harmony at school, at home, or wherever they may be. Terrence wrote, "I'm a peacemaker now. I never let my brother down." Children start to become aware of reality as process they can affect, and this awareness is reinforced by their writing.

Educational theorist Lev Vygotsky said that we internalize other people's language and make it our own. What we take in we often give out. Our thoughts are based on things we've heard, seen, or read. Thoughts lead to dialogue, which is validated by writing. The combination often culminates in action. The words we speak and write give way to new thoughts, new dialogue, broader perceptions. Thus the cycle is actually broader and more synergistic than I had first envisioned.

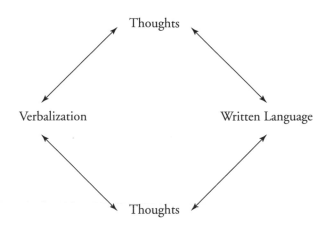

The purpose of peacemaking is to enable future adults to move beyond the paradigm that enables prejudice, discrimination, violence and war to exist. It is, in truth the work of transformation, and it is my hope that new understandings, culled and honed through speaking and writing, will lead children to new paths of action. What actions might they take? Perhaps they will become more humane, reflective individuals for whom respect and conciliation will be an unshakable part of their lives. Perhaps they will refuse to tolerate violence through words or behaviors. Perhaps they will begin to challenge the status quo. As Freire says, "History is not finished yet." The work we do today with children has the capacity to have an impact on the future. We must choose wisely what we teach.

PART Three

Integrating Literature and Peacemaking: A Primary Unit

Literature entices, motivates, and instructs. It opens doors to discovery. . . .
—Donna Norton, 4

I n this section you will find eleven lessons that use literature to reinforce peacemaking skills, giving children a feeling of connectedness to the larger world. These lessons help to motivate children to apply peacemaking in their daily lives as they learn about taking responsibility for their actions, caring for the earth, and resolving conflicts.

Why Use Literature?

Children learn much from themes and characters in books. Louise Rosenblatt in her groundbreaking book *Literature as Exploration* said:

> The whole personality tends to become involved in the literary experience. That a literary work may bring into play and be related to profoundly personal needs and preoccupations makes it a powerful potential educational force. For it is out of these basic needs and attitudes that behavior springs. (183)

Rosenblatt strongly believed literature could help us reach crucial goals in our society. She said, "More than ever, we need to foster the growth of people who will have the inner strength and the humane values needed to face constructively these times of crucial decisions and awesome yet wonderful possibilities" (xiv). Teachers must use every tool at their disposal to help children develop humane values and the means to live by them throughout their lives. Literature can be a powerful vehicle toward this end.

By examining conflicts in books, children can learn valuable lessons that later can be applied to real-life situations. Repeatedly I have heard children talk about characters in books as though they were real, offering advice and speculating as to how the characters can solve their problems. When subsequently faced with a similar real-life problem, children can cull from thinking that they have already done through the lives of story characters. Thus, a more solid framework for dealing with problems is created.

The National Council of Teacher's of English (NCTE) devoted an edition of *Primary Voices* to the matter of conflict resolution, stressing the importance of bringing conflict resolution skills to the classroom. They recommended using children's books for this purpose, urging teachers toward the practice of "helping students learn how to solve conflicts themselves by focusing on the conflicts located in children's literature" (9). What better way is there to expose children to new ways of thinking than through wonderful books?

Robert Coles in *The Call of Stories* said, "a compelling narrative, offering a storyteller's moral imagination vigorously at work, can enable any of us to learn by example, to take to heart what really is a gift of grace" (191).

What Books Are Included in this Unit?

The first book included in this unit is an exquisitely illustrated picture book called *Dear Children of the Earth*, by Schim Shimmel. A plea for reverence toward the earth that sustains us, this book begins with the words, "Dear Children of the Earth, I am writing to ask for your help"(1). Mother Earth then speaks; and as she does, we see her as a beautiful but fragile part of the universe. Her letter to us ends with the words, "Remember, I am your Home. And just like you, there is only one of me" (30).

The technique of the earth speaking, coupled with Schimmel's magnificent illustrations, makes this a very powerful book, appropriate for people of all ages. It carries the same message as another excellent picture book, *Natural History*, by M. B. Goffstein, which is now out of print but available through the Internet (Amazon, com). You may want to use the following passage from Goffstein's book when introducing *Dear Children of the Earth*.

> Every living creature is our brother
> and our sister, dearer than the jewels
> at the center of the earth. So let us
> be like tiny grains of sand and protect
> all life from fear and suffering! Then,
> when the stars shine, we can sleep in peace. . . .
> (Goffstein, 19-23)

Dear Children of the Earth will not only help children see themselves as part of a larger world, it also will enable them to understand why they need to take care of the earth with diligence.

The next book is *Peace on the Playground, Nonviolent Ways of Problem-Solving*, a nonfiction book by Eileen Lucas. It provides a global perspective as well as practical suggestions for solving common problems that arise among children. We learn one child's definition of peace as, " . . . people talking together with a heart in between them," (9); and it is with heart and care that Lucas brings to life many peacemaking concepts. She highlights communicating, negotiating, the meaning of nonviolence, the issue of prejudice, the nature of conflict, and each

person's role in making our world a better place. Lucas helps children see that we all need to make positive, humane choices; and she teaches us how this can be done.

Powerful lessons in resolving conflicts nonviolently are learned through *The Secret of the Peaceful Warrior* by Dan Millman. In this book (featured in Chapter 1), a boy named Danny is confronted by the school bully. He ultimately learns how to overcome his fear and face the bully with strength and dignity, eventually becoming his friend. This book is an excellent springboard for discussing alternatives to violence and the challenges children confront when they consider meeting aggressive behavior with nonaggressive strength.

My Song Is Beautiful, Poems and Pictures in Many Voices, compiled by Mary Ann Hoberman, has many excellent poems. Two are particularly relevant to peacemaking. "Who Am I?" reinforces a child's place in the world, and "You and I" introduces the concept that people are all the same inside.

The Quarreling Book by Charlotte Zolotow, an endearing picture book, illustrated by Arnold Lobel, shows how our actions affect those around us. When Mr. James neglects to kiss Mrs. James before going to work, Mrs. James then snaps at Jonathan James, who snaps, in turn, at his sister. The chain reaction continues until a child's puppy reverses the negative course of events. Readers then see what happens as each of these characters reacts positively to the others. **The Quarreling Book** is a most delightful way to show children the impact our actions have upon one another.

A far more serious look at the impact of peoples' actions upon others is the biography *Rosa Parks*, by Eloise Greenfield. This important book shows Rosa Parks's courage in the face of prejudice and her ability to stand up for her convictions against seemingly insurmountable circumstances. Parks, having grown up in the

Deep South was witness to and victim of countless incidences of racial bias. After seeing a fifteen-year-old girl forced off a bus in handcuffs for refusing to sit in the back, Rosa Parks decided she would allow this no more. The following week, she refused to give up her seat to a white man. Her subsequent arrest was the defining moment that gave birth to the Civil Rights Movement. Parks's biography tells a story of bravery and hope in the face of inhumanity. There are many lessons for children to learn here.

We All Make a Difference:
Dear Children of the Earth

Objectives

1. The children will be able to understand the author's message: The earth is our home and we must take care of it.
2. The children will define what peace means to them.
3. The children will be introduced to the following definition of peace: "Peace means taking care of ourselves, each other, and our Earth." (Drew, 27)
4. Children will examine their role in taking care of the earth and its inhabitants.

Materials

1. Globe.
2. Book, *Dear Children of the Earth.*
3. Blank chart paper (four sheets) and a marker.
4. Chart containing the definition of peace.

Procedure

1. Have children gather in a circle on the floor. Show the globe and tell the children that they will hear a story about Earth and some of the people who inhabit it. Say, "The author has an important message for you in this book. See if you can discover what it is."
2. Read the book, *Dear Children of the Earth.*
3. Discuss, eliciting from the children responses to the following questions.
   • What do you think the author was trying to tell us?
   • What are the beautiful things you noticed about the earth in this story?
   • What are some of the sad things you noticed in the story?
   • What do you think the author meant by saying, "The animals have told me, 'We are worried, Mother Earth'"?
   • Mother Earth asks us, "What do you think I need from you more than anything else in the world?" What do you think it is? How can we help?
4. Say, "By taking care of the earth and all its creatures, we can help make it a more peaceful place. What does peace mean to you? Discuss in detail, listing the children's responses on chart paper.
5. Say, "There are many definitions of peace. Here's one that many people have used."

Show chart with the definition, "Peace means taking care of ourselves, each other, and our Earth." Discuss, allowing children to see that one way people care for others is by treating them with kindness and respect and working out differences that arise between us.

6. Have children give examples of ways we can take care of ourselves, each other, and Earth. On chart paper, list examples the children give.

7. Conclude the lesson by telling the children that tomorrow they will paint a large mural of the earth; then, each child will add a tag (sentence strip) saying how one person one person can make a difference. Say, "Tonight I would like you to think of one thing you yourself can do to show care for people, other living things or the Earth." Briefly discuss the children's suggestions, making sure they understand the concept.

Ways We Make a Difference

Objectives

1. The children will each define one way that a person can make a difference in showing care for other people, living things, or the earth.
2. The class will collaborate in small groups to paint a mural of the earth and its people. (A parent, aide, or upper-grade child may be needed to help with painting.)
3. The children will show an understanding of why it's important to take responsibility for caring about others and the earth.

Materials

1. Large mural paper (4 feet by 7 feet, minimum). Roughly sketch Earth on the paper.
2. Tempera paints in different colors (especially blue and green), paint brushes, newspaper.
3. Smocks.
4. Globe.
5. Sentence strips—one for each child and one for you.
6. Markers.
7. Definition of "peace" from Lesson 1.
8. Blue and green clay, enough so that each child can make a small "Earth."
9. Poem titled "Who Am I?" written on chart paper. You will find this poem in the book, *My Song is Beautiful,* by Mary Ann Hoberman.
10. Also from *My Song Is Beautiful,* the poem "You and I" on chart paper.

Procedure

1. Have the children gather in a circle around the globe. Say, "What did we discover was the author's message in *Dear Children of the Earth?*" That we all need to do our share in taking care of the earth and its inhabitants). Discuss briefly.
2. Direct the children's attention to the globe. Remind the children that Earth is shared by many different peoples. It's essential for each of us to treat others with kindness and respect. Point out that each land mass represents a place where people live. Briefly discuss the land masses and oceans they will be painting. Tell the children that they are going to make a mural to hang in the hall. The entire school will see and learn from it. Remind them that their sentence strips will go around the mural.
3. Review the definition of *peace* from yesterday's lesson and discuss briefly.

4. Ask each child to share the idea he or she came up with to show care for the earth, its people, and other living things. Discuss.

5. Divide the children into groups of four. Tell them that each group will have a turn to paint the mural, write their ideas on sentence strips (or have an adult do it for them), and make an "Earth" out of clay.

6. Have a helper supervise the painting of the mural with one group at a time, while you supervise the other groups writing sentence strips and making clay Earth models.

7. To complete this lesson, have each child hang his or her sentence strip around the mural. Read each strip aloud as it is added. Hang the mural in the hall with the title, "We May Be Small, but We Make a Big Difference." Clay "Earths" can be displayed on a table in the room. End by reading and discussing "Who am I?"

Introducing Conflict Resolution:
The Secret of the Peaceful Warrior

Objectives

1. The children will learn the meaning of *conflict*.
2. The children will brainstorm solutions for the conflict in the story.
3. The children will be introduced to the Win/Win Guidelines for resolving conflict

Materials

1. Book, *The Secret of the Peaceful Warrior*
2. The Win/Win Guidelines on a large chart and a copy for each child to take home. (see page 14)
3. Three or four pieces of blank sheets of chart paper for brainstorming.
4. Markers.

Procedure

1. Introduce *The Secret of the Peaceful Warrior* by asking if any of the children have ever been in a group in which members were fighting with each other. Ask what happened. Discuss briefly.
2. Review the definition of the word *conflict*. Tell the children that conflicts are a normal part of life, but often the way conflicts are handled creates more problems. Discuss.

3. Introduce the concept of choice, saying, "People have conflicts; it's part of being human. What matters most is the choices we make when conflicts arise. We can choose to do negative things, like hitting, punching, yelling, or name-calling; but when we make choices like these, what usually happens?" Guide children to the understanding that negative choices make conflicts worse. Help them name some of the negative outcomes that derive from negative choices (e.g., loss of friends, getting in trouble at school, disappointing our parents, feeling ashamed of what we did, gaining a reputation as a troublemaker, subsequent fights that can emerge from the initial conflict, and even escalation into violence.)
4. Now ask the children, "What are positive choices we can make in the face of conflict?" Guide them to see the following positive choice: I can use my words instead of fists, walk away with my head held high, implying that "this isn't worth fighting over." Also, we can ask a peer mediator or an adult for help. We can cool off and talk out the problem when we're not so mad. Remind the children that when we allow someone to make us so angry that we choose to fight, **we've lost**.

When you fight, you've let your feelings get out of control. Say, "It takes more courage to stand tall with dignity and walk away." Emphasize the difference between walking away tall and strong and walking away defeated and "wimpy." Urge your students to view walking away as the bravest thing they can do—just like Martin Luther King, Jr., told millions of people.

5. Say, "I'm going to read you a story about a boy named Danny who learned about true courage in the face of conflict. Let's find out what positive choices he made when confronted by a bully.

   Read the story; then ask the following questions.
   - What did Danny do to make himself feel less fearful of the bully?
   - How did the bully react when Danny found a way to stand up to him without fighting?
   - What might have happened if Danny had chosen to fight?

- What can you do if you ever get into a situation like Danny's?

7. Say, "You've all learned how to use the Win/Win Guidelines. Let's see what might have happened if Danny were able to use these guidelines with the bully. Let's replay the conflict and then imagine that when Danny goes to school, instead of hiding, he asks his teacher to help him work out the problem with the bully.

8. Have the children act out the resolution of conflict in the story, using the Win/Win Guidelines. You can pick a child to play the role of teacher, or you can do so yourself.

   Talk about the outcome. Conclude by reminding the children that *we always have a choice when there's a conflict*. Distribute copies of the Win/Win Guidelines. For homework, have the children review the guidelines with their parents. Remind the children to use these guidelines at home as well as in school.

LESSON *4*

Role Playing Solutions to Conflicts

Objectives

1. The children will review and show an understanding of the Win/Win Guidelines for resolving conflicts.
2. The children will demonstrate their understanding of the guidelines through role playing.
3. The children will show an understanding of the concept that being a peacemaker means being willing to work out conflicts rather than fighting.

Materials

1. *The Secret of the Peaceful Warrior* .
2. Chart with the Win/Win Guidelines.
3. Blank chart paper for brainstorming.
4. Markers.
5. Definition of peace.
6. Two puppets.

Procedure

1. Gather the children in a circle. Refer to yesterday's story, *The Secret of the Peaceful Warrior.* Ask the children what important lessons they learned from this book. Discuss.

2. Tell the children that today they'll be acting out conflicts they've had in their lives. Say, "Before we do this, I need you to help resolve a conflict that happened this morning." Have the puppets tell the story of a fight they had over a toy. Have the first puppet say that the second one grabbed the toy away from him. Have the first puppet admit that he got so angry he hit the other one. Have the puppet show remorse for striking out in anger, but also have him state that he didn't know what else to do.

3. Ask the children to brainstorm solutions to this conflict. List their solutions on the chart paper. When you have gathered at least ten solutions, ask the puppets to choose a solution they can both agree on.

4. Next, have the puppets replay their conflict using the Win/Win Guidelines. Have the children *coach* the puppets as to which step to use each time.

5. Review "I messages." Practice giving "I messages" with the children, making sure they understand how to give one without placing blame.

6. Ask the class if anyone has had a conflict they would like to role-play for the class. Listen to

a few conflicts and choose one for role-playing. You can play one role and have a child play the other.

7. After the conflict has been acted out, replay it using the Win/Win Guidelines. Have all the children give solutions when you get to step 5 (brainstorming solutions).

8. On completion, ask the children how working out conflicts helps us be peacemakers. Refer to the definition of *peace* and remind the children that when we work things out rather than fight, we're showing care for others and ourselves. Remind the children of the lesson learned by Danny in *The Secret of the Peaceful Warrior*.

Peace on the Playground

NOTE: This lesson should be followed up the next day.

Objectives

1. The children will distinguish between violent and nonviolent actions.
2. The children will understand that name-calling is a form of abusive behavior and is not acceptable.
3. The children will show an understanding that use of the Win/Win Guidelines is always preferable to name-calling and violence.

Materials

1. *Peace on the Playground,* Chapter 2, "Violence and Conflict."
2. Puppets from Lesson 4.
3. Two sheets of chart paper.
4. Markers.
5. The Win/Win Guidelines.

Procedure

1. Gather the children in a circle. Acknowledge them for the good job they did in the previous lesson when they role-played solutions to conflicts. Tell them that today you will be reading to them from a book called *Peace on the Playground,* which talks about real conflict situations.
2. Ask the class if they know what the word "violence" means. Discuss, and then define violence as any act that causes physical or emotional harm to another person or to oneself. Ask the children to give examples of things they know to be violent (fighting, name-calling, etc.). Encourage them to list examples they have seen on TV, in movies, and on video games as well.
3. Turn to page 18 of *Peace on the Playground,* which shows children embroiled in a fight. Ask, "What makes people fight?" Discuss, emphasizing that people always have choices when they are angry, and that fighting is a negative choice.
4. Say, "Fighting is a form of violence. When people choose to work out their differences instead of fighting, they are choosing to act in a way that is nonviolent. (Write "nonviolent" on board.)
5. Tell the children that you're going to read something that will help them learn more

about nonviolent choices. Read Chapter 2
(Peace on the Playground).

6. Ask the following questions.
   - Is conflict in itself bad? (No)
   - What is bad about conflict? (The way we sometimes choose to handle it.)
   - Why do people often respond to conflict violently? (They don't know they have other alternatives.)
   - What word describes actions we choose that are not violent? (Nonviolence.)
   - How do **you** usually deal with conflict?
   - Is there a better way?

7. Say, "Now I'm going to tell you the story of the two children pictured in the book.

   Jeffrey and Kenneth were playing kickball. When Jeffrey saw a pop fly ball coming toward him, he ran for it as fast as he could. Kenneth was doing the same. They crashed into each other by mistake, but Jeffrey was so angry that he punched Kenneth in the stomach. Then Kenneth got so mad he punched Jeffrey back. Before long both boys were in a big fight. They ended up being sent to the principal's office. What could Jeffrey and Kenneth have done differently? Have the children brainstorm as many solutions as possible.

8. On chart paper, list the children's solutions. Encourage them to refer to the Win/Win Guidelines.

9. After listing a wide variety of solutions, have the class decide which solution or combination of solutions would be best. Remind the children that as peacemakers we need to show care for others by the choices we make during conflicts, even if we're angry.

10. End by reviewing why nonviolent choices are always preferable. Talk about ways that children can redirect their anger. Have the children tell ways they can cool off when angry as you list them on the board. Stress that anger itself is not bad. It's what we sometimes choose to do with our anger that can be bad. Say, "When we cool off, we can think more clearly and can make better choices in the face of anger."

11. Assign the following homework. Say, "I want you to notice what kinds of things make you angry. Next time you feel angry enough to fight, I want you to try cooling off and then working out the conflict with the Win/Win Guidelines. Tomorrow we will discuss the outcome."

    NOTE: Be sure to leave ample time the next day for follow up. When you do, encourage the children to discuss what they noticed about their anger triggers. See how many were successful in resolving their conflicts.

Our Actions Make a Difference: *The Quarreling Book*

Objectives

1. The children will learn that their actions affect the people in their lives.
2. The children will experience the lighter side of peacemaking, seeing the humor in the story as well as the lesson it teaches.
3. The children will understand that everyone has feelings.

Materials

1. *The Quarreling Book.*
2. Two puppets.
3. Poem "You and I" (from Lesson 2) on chart paper.

Procedure

1. Have the children gather in a circle. Hold up the puppets. Have one puppet tell the children that his or her feelings were hurt when a friend refused to play. Have the children respond. The other puppet can tell about a time he/she felt hurt when a friend wouldn't share crayons. Again, let the children respond.
2. Ask the children to remember their own hurt feelings. Discuss.
3. Ask, "How did you react?" Discuss.
4. Tell the children that you will read them a story about how one person's hurt feelings affected everyone else's day.
5. Read *The Quarreling Book.*
6. Ask these questions. [Bulleted list]
   • What made Mrs. James upset?
   • What happened next?
   • Continue asking the same question until you have elicited the entire chain of events.
   • What changed everything around?
   • Did the story have a happy ending? Why?
7. Have the children act out the story.
8. Ask, "What lesson did you learn from this book? Discuss.
9. End with the reading of "You and I," focusing on the fact that everyone in the world has feelings. Tell the children that tomorrow they're going to make a "web" of the events in *The Quarreling Book.*

The Quarreling Web

Objectives

1. The children will recall the sequence and details of *The Quarreling Book*.
2. The children will help make a large web of the story.
3. The children will recall that their actions affect those around them.

Materials

1. *The Quarreling Book*.
2. Large paper for making a web of the story.
3. Markers.
4. A sheet of manila paper for each child.
5. Crayons.

Procedure

1. Refer to *The Quarreling Book*. Say, "We're going to make a web of details of the story in the order they happened."
2. Hang the large paper on the board. Ask the children to start at the beginning and tell you each detail of the story. Write down their sentences, webbing in a circular fashion so the chain of events is obvious upon completion. Leave room above each sentence for matching pictures to be drawn by the children.
3. Discuss the web when it is completed. Now have the children reenact the story, this time having Mr. Martin kiss Mrs. Martin good-bye before leaving the house.
4. End by reiterating how each person's action makes a difference. Emphasize the necessity to show care for others.

LESSON 8

The Story of Rosa Parks

Objectives

1. The children will gain an understanding of racial prejudice.
2. The children will understand how one person's courageous actions can make a huge difference.
3. The children will understand that even in the face of hatred, we need to make nonviolent choices, as Rosa Parks did.
4. The children will understand that being a peacemaker is not always easy, but it's the right thing to do.

Materials

1. *Rosa Parks* by Eloise Greenfield.
2. Chalkboard, chalk.

Procedure

1. Write the words "prejudice" and discrimination on the board. Ask the children if they know these words. Discuss and define them.
2. Tell the children that the world has many different peoples. Some people know about being peacemakers; others don't. Let the children know that today you'll read a true story about a brave woman named Rosa Parks, who chose peaceful actions even when those around her did not, and that through this story they'll come to understand how Rosa chose to handle prejudice and discrimination.
3. Read the story of Rosa Parks.
4. Ask the following questions:
   - What brave choice did Rosa make?
   - How did her choice affect others?
   - What would you have done if you had been in Rosa's shoes?
   - How was racial prejudice evidenced?
   - How did it make you feel when you learned about how Rosa Parks and other blacks were treated?
   - What important lessons can we learn from Rosa Parks?
5. Give the children plenty of time to discuss the upsetting aspects of this story. Examine the affects of prejudice and discrimination upon the people of Rosa Parks' s era.
6. Ask the children if they are aware of any forms of prejudice that exist today.
7. End by reminding the children that we always have choices and that to be peacemakers, we must always make choices that show care and respect for others.

Creating a Book About Rosa Parks

Objectives

1. The children will review the details in and their understanding of Rosa Parks's biography.
2. The children will create a stand-up book about Rosa Parks.

Materials

1. *Rosa Parks*, the book.
2. Approximately 20 sheets of oak tag for pages in the stand up book.
3. Masking tape to attach oak tag in the following manner:

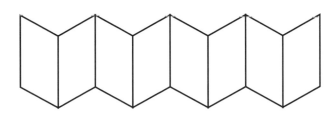

4. Markers and crayons.

Procedure

1. Review the book, *Rosa Parks*. Have children retell the story including all major details. On the board, list about twenty of the most important details.
2. On the board, draw the format for the stand-up book the children will create.
3. Assign one story detail per child, or per pair if you have over twenty in your class. Each child or pair of children will illustrate their assigned detail on oak tag. Have them write or dictate a sentence, or caption, below the their illustrations.
4. On completion, arrange the details (sheets of oak tag) in proper sequence.
5. Have the children take turns reading the book they have just made. Invite other classes to come in and listen.

Planning a Peace Day Celebration

Objectives

1. The children will take part in planning Children's Peace Day Celebration based on the literature you have read.
2. The children will review and reiterate the key concepts they have learned throughout this unit.
3. The children will take jobs in preparing for the celebration.

Materials

1. Chart paper on which to list the children's ideas for the celebration, and assigned tasks.
2. Poems, "You and I" and "Who Am I?"
3. Charts: The Win/Win Guidelines, definition of peace.

Procedure

1. Ask the children if they would like to have a Children's Peace Day to celebrate what they have learned and share it with their parents.
2. Ask the children the types of things they would like to do for their celebration. Remind them that whatever they choose to do should demonstrate things they have learned about peacemaking.
3. If the children don't suggest some of the following activities, you can suggest any or all of them.
   - Read the book they made about Rosa Parks.
   - Memorize the poems you've read and recite them in small groups.
   - Present the Earth mural and read our ideas for showing care for the Earth.
   - Role-play the resolution of a conflict through the Win/Win Guidelines.
   - Act out *The Quarreling Book*.
3. Ask the children what refreshments they want to have at the celebration. Suggest that each child bring in a dish relating to his or her ethnic origins.
4. Ask if the children know any songs they might want to sing. One excellent choice is "We All Live Together" (Youngheart Records).
5. List all decisions on charts. Assign tasks. Draft a note to parents announcing the date and time of the celebration. Invite them to bring an ethnic dish.

6. Divide children into groups and assign performance roles to each group; e.g. poem recitation group, role-playing group.

7. End by planning rehearsal time. You also may want to have the children make colorful invitations to their parents to go along with your note. Why not invite the principal, too? Invite the local newspapers to cover Children's Peace Day. They'll appreciate it.

Culminating Activity: Children's Peace Day

Objectives

1. The class celebrates what they have learned from the books about peacemaking.
2. The children reiterate the major understandings they have gained.
3. The children share their expanded insights and knowledge with their parents through their performances.

Materials

1. Definition of peace and Win/Win Guidelines.
2. Charts containing the two poems ("Who Am I?" and "You and I").
3. Rosa Parks stand-up book.
4. Earth mural.
5. Story web: *The Quarreling Book*.
6. Foods to be served, serving table, utensils, plates, napkins, and cups.
7. Extra chairs for parents.

Procedure

1. Welcome parents and give them some background on what the children have been learning.
2. Have the children point out charts hanging around the room and tell briefly what each chart means.
3. Have performance groups give their presentations.
4. End this portion of the festivities with the song you have selected.
5. Ask the parents to tell about any ethnic dishes they have brought.
6. Share the refreshments—enjoy!
7. When the celebration is complete, see if you can display the children's projects in the library or other visible spot for the whole school to see.
8. Affirm all the children (and yourself!) for the wonderful celebration.
9. Give students a copy of this poem ("Not Alone") and time to read it silently and think about it. Or read it to them orally as they listen.

NOT ALONE

Be my brother,
be my sister,
We can't live alone.

Skin of brown
or white or yellow,
We can't live alone.

I see a boy
who's in a wheelchair,
Let me push it for him.

That girl who speaks
another language,
Help me understand her.

Be my brother,
be my sister,
Let's not live apart.

We all come
from different places,
open up your heart.

Brothers, sisters,
seek each other.
Hear your many voices.

Move beyond
the separations.
Let's all make new choices.

by Naomi Drew

Appendix

All Grades

Creating a Peaceful Classroom

Objectives

- The teacher and students will create the setting for a peaceful classroom.
- The students will list qualities of a peaceful classroom.

Materials

- Two large pieces of chart paper
- Markers
- Copies of the Parent letter (see page 51)
- "Friends" (see page 52)

Procedure

1. Think of every child in your class as whole, perfect, and capable. Focus on the promise of each child and imagine this year being the realization of this promise. Also, think about the promise of you, as teacher, impacting your students for the rest of their lives out of the way you interact with them this year. Think of your students as responsible, productive, and caring individuals. Know that you have the ability to help them develop in this way. Now you are ready to have a dialogue with your students.

2. Ask students to sit in a circle either on the floor or in chairs. The circle connects them visually and allows them to see one another. It is helpful to have a permanent space in the room where you can easily form a circle.

3. Say, "Out of my care for you, I want to find new ways to have a peaceful future. We often hear about people hurting each other or not caring about one another. I started to picture what the world would be like if teachers everywhere began to teach their students how to get along and accept other people. What kind of world would it be? Peace starts with each individual, and the way you act affects the world around you." Allow the children to respond.

4. Express your interest in getting to know each student and your willingness to be there for them if they have a problem. You might say something like, "I want us to have a great year together. Out of our cooperation and care for one another we can all help to make this happen."

5. Speak about the need for everyone in the class to work as partners, to cooperate, and to be considerate. Discuss the meaning of the word "considerate." Stress the need for each member to take responsibility for

having a peaceful atmosphere in the class. Ask, "What does taking responsibility mean to you?" Discuss.

6. Ask, "How do you want it to be in our room throughout the year? How do you want to be treated and how do you want to treat others?" You can begin by stating some of the ways you would like the class to be. (Example: I want the children to be considerate of one another.)

7. After the children have discussed the kind of class atmosphere they want, you can label this atmosphere as "peaceful." On a piece of chart paper write: A Peaceful Classroom Is One in Which . . .

8. Ask your students to reiterate the qualities of a peaceful classroom on the chart. It may start something like this: "A peaceful classroom is one in which . . . we are considerate of each other. We speak quietly. We pay attention when someone else is speaking. We don't call each other names." You can keep expanding this chart throughout the year.

9. After you complete the chart together, ask the children what a "non-peaceful" classroom might be like. Discuss. Ask what it would take, on the part of each student, to have the class be the way they want it to be. Discuss.

10. Ask your students if they will all agree to do whatever it takes to create a peaceful classroom and bring to life what they listed on the chart. Tell them that the chart can serve as a guide to follow during the year, and that additions can be made to it at any time.

11. Ask if anyone feels that they might have a problem abiding by the "rules" one the chart. Discuss. Stress the need for cooperation and the fact that everyone working together will make a huge difference.

12. Ask the class to sign an agreement which states, "We agree to follow the rules we created together to have a peaceful classroom." Hang this next to the "A Peaceful Classroom Is One in Which . . ." chart.

13. Copy the Peaceful Classroom chart and send it home to your students' parents with a note (suggested wording on page 117).

14. Discuss the note with your class. Ask them to discuss it and the chart rules with their families for homework.

15. Conclude by reading "Friends" (see page 118).

LESSON *1*

Dear Parent(s),

Our class has developed a set of rules (attached) which we have all agreed to follow throughout the year. We invite you to be our partners in the goal of having a peaceful classroom this year. Would you save these rules and talk them over with me?

Throughout the year we'll be doing other activities like this from a program called *The Peaceful Classroom in Action.* In this program we are learning that peace starts with each individual, and that it's important for all of use to take responsibility for our actions.

If you have any questions about the program, or our rules for a peaceful classroom, my teacher would be happy to speak to you.

Thanks very much.

Child's Name

by Jonathan Sprout

Have you ever travelled far away to another town?
Did you feel like a stranger when you were there?
It's just a state of mind. You can feel at home anywhere.
Anywhere you go, there are kids who care.
There are no towns full of bad people.
In every town there are good people.
And just like you and me
They wish we all were friends.
Far away in countries all around the world
There are millions of people we may never see.
But they're reaching out and they're opening up their hearts.
And they want to be friends with you and me.
There are no countries full of bad people.
In every country there are good people.
And just like you and me
They wish that we were friends.
Everywhere you look today
People want to give.
It doesn't matter what they say,
We all should live
As friends!
No matter where we live
Or what language we speak
No matter what religion we believe in
No matter how we dress
Or what lifestyle we seek
No matter the color of our skin.

Grades K-2

Resolving Conflicts— "The Quick Method" (K-2)

Objectives

- To introduce the basics of conflict resolution
- To guide the children to understand the benefits of resolving conflicts peacefully.

Materials

- Puppets
- Chalkboard
- Chart:

Quick WIN/WIN

1. Cool off
2. "I Message"
3. Brainstorm solutions
4. Affirm, forgive, thank

Procedure

1. Have the children form a circle on the floor. Introduce the puppets. Tell the children that the puppets are having a disagreement or conflict over a toy that they want.

   Have the puppets act out the conflict: grab at each other, call each other names, cry, or whatever else your imagination comes up with.

2. Speak directly to the puppets. Ask each puppet to state the problem. Don't let the puppets interrupt each other. Let them know that each will get a turn.

3. Help the puppets understand others' "point of view." Teach them how to use "I Messages."

4. Ask the children to brainstorm solutions to the puppets' conflict. List all their suggestions on the board.

5. Talk to the puppets again and have them choose a solution that satisfies them both. Have the puppets thank the class for helping them work it out.

6. Have the puppets ask the children why it's better to work it out then fight it out; discuss.

7. Have the puppets ask the children about conflicts they have had. Discuss the brainstorming solutions together. Choose the most viable. Go over giving "I Messages" at this time.

8. Ask the children if they would be willing to try working out their problems this way in order to create the peaceful class they would like to have.

9. Go over the above chart with the class.

LESSON *3*

Grades 3-6

Resolving Conflicts— "The Quick Method" (3–6)

Objectives

- To introduce the basics of conflict resolution.
- To guide the children to understand the benefits of resolving conflicts peacefully.

Materials

- Clipboard
- Chart of Quick "Win/Win"
- Large blank chart paper and marker

Quick WIN/WIN

1. Cool off
2. "I Message"
3. Brainstorm solutions
4. Affirm, forgive, thank

Procedure

1. Introduce the lesson by staging a conflict with another staff person over an unreturned book. Have the other person storm out.
2. Students will respond. Ask for suggestions as to how to work out the conflict. Elicit as many ideas as possible. List them on large chart paper.

3. Let the children know that what they just saw was a staged conflict. Say, "In our class this year, when we have a problem with another person, instead of becoming enemies we are going to try to work things out."
4. Say, "I am going to teach you a quick way to work conflicts out. Later in our peacemaking program you will learn to work problems out in more detail." (Go over chart with class. Emphasize "I Messages." Give examples of it.)
5. Listen to conflicts the children have had and have students play act with the "quick method."
6. Say, "When you have conflict that you can't seem to resolve yourself and I'm busy, you can list them on our clipboard. [Show, and tell where it will hang.] You list the date, the names of the people involved, and briefly describe the problem. Include your signature. A number of times a week, I'll take the clipboard problems and we will help each other as a group to work them out."
7. Say, "What would our class be like if everybody was willing to talk and work out their problems?"
8. Say, "What would the world be like if government leaders did the same?"

All Grades

Using "I Messages"

NOTE: Refer to *Parent Effectiveness Training*, by Thomas Gordon, or *Effectiveness Training for Women* by Linda Evans before doing this lesson. giving I messages" is a complex communication technique. These books will help.

Objectives

- The children will role play problems that lead to conflict.
- The children will learn to use "I Messages" in conflict situations

---

I Messages

I feel angry.

I'm sad because you took my toy.

I'm embarrassed because you called me
a name.

You Messages

You're a pain.

You're mean.

You make me mad.

Materials

- "I Messages/You Messages" poster

Procedure

1. Have the children sit in a circle. Say, "Today we're going to do a fun relaxation exercise to start our lesson." Say, "Close your eyes and picture a great big scoop of your favorite ice cream. Put it on top of our favorite cone— sugar or wafer. Now put another scoop on top. Take a lick. Feel the cold smoothness of it on your tongue. Swallow the ice cream. Feel it going down your throat and into your stomach. Feel the coldness. Now take another lick and then a big bite. Feel the coldness on your teeth. Now, eat the whole thing. You're full now, rub your stomach and smile."

2. Say, "Now that you're all full, we're going to talk about something you can do when you have a conflict which will help you work out your differences.

3. Say, "What we're going to talk about is called 'I Messages.' There are two ways people can speak when they are talking

about their feelings. People can start with either the word 'I' or 'You.'"

4. Say, "When you start with the word 'I' you don't place blame on others. 'I Messages' show that you are responsible for the way you feel. When you start with the word 'I' you don't put the other person on the defensive." Explain. Say "Remember, we all are responsible for your own feelings." Discuss.

5. Ask the students to look at the chart with 'I/You Messages." Have a student read it aloud. Explain that "You Messages" put other people on the defensive and make them less likely to want to solve conflicts.

6. Set up some imaginary conflict situations. Have students first use "You Messages," then "I Messages." Ask which worked better. Discuss. Encourage full participation. Thank the children who participate.

7. Students will role play the following situations, first as they wold normally handle it, then using "I Messages."

   a. There is a pencil on the floor. Two people go to pick it up at once. They start to argue over whose pencil it is.

   b. Tom and Jason are walking to lunch. Mike asks if he can join them. Tom and Jason ignore Mike. Mike feels hurt.

   c. Maria and Peggy are working on a project together. Peggy hasn't brought the materials she is responsible for. Now the project might have to be turned in late.

   d. Alan's friend yelled at him this morning on the playground Alan comes to school sad and upset. When another fried, Dave, says hello to him in line, Alan says "Get out of here!"

   After each role play, discuss what worked better, the "old way" or using "I Messages."

   NOTE: Giving "I Messages" is tricky. You might need to have your students practice it a few times before they get the hang of it.

8. Come up with other situations where the children can practice using "I Messages." Give them time to practice.

9. Ask, "How do you suppose this could work with countries who don't get along.

10. Ask, "Do you think it's possible for nations to work out their differences through talking to one another?"

11. Ask, "Do you think it's worth the extra effort for nations to try this? Why?"

All Grades

Defining Peace

Objectives

- The children will explore personal meanings of peace.
- The children will learn one definition of peace "Peace means taking care of ourselves, each others, and our earth."
- The children will learn that peace is personal but also denotes a sense of responsibility and a commitment to others and the environment.

Materials

- Large paper with words written on it in bright letters: "What Peace Feels Like to Me"
- "Peace means taking care of ourselves, each other, and our earth" on a poster
- Posters or pictures from magazines showing the following.
  a. People taking care of themselves (emotional and physical well-being)
  b. People taking care of each other (love, assistance)
  c. People taking care of the earth (environment)
- Posters or pictures showing the result of people not taking care of themselves, one another, the earth. Children can bring these in ahead of time.

- Drawing paper and crayons for young children. Writing paper and pencils (for older children).
  NOTE: This lesson correlates with Bulletin Board, entitled "Peace Means Taking Care of Ourselves, Each Other, and Our Earth."

Procedure

1. Have the children sit in a circle.
2. Say, "In order to create a calm and peaceful atmosphere in our classroom, we are first going to get very still and take some deep breaths. Let your body relax. Let a warm, calm, peaceful feeling flow through every part of you, from the tips of your toes to the top of your head. Listen to your own breathing. Listen to the perfect silence and calmness in our room. Now take a moment and think about what peace feels like to you." Give students a moment of silence in which to do this.
3. Say, "What does peace feel like to you?" On the large paper entitled "What Peace Feels Like to Me," record their answers. Accept anything, but try to guide your students away from the stereotyped concepts of peace. This exercise allows students to explore their beliefs and feelings about peace.

4. Ask, "What does peace look like to you? How does this room look when it's peaceful? How does your home and the people in it look when they are peaceful? How does your street or neighborhood look when it is peaceful? How do you think our earth would look if it were peaceful?" Discuss. Encourage lots of participation. Acknowledge each child's response. Continue to guide your children away from the stereotyped meanings of peace. Allow them to draw from their own experiences of peacefulness.

5. Say, "Here is one definition of peace: 'Peace means taking care of ourselves, each other, and our earth.'" Show the sign you have made with these words on it. Be sure this is written in large, bright letters. This will serve as a sign to be displayed in the room.

6. Ask a child to read the sign aloud. Discuss.

7. Show pictures of people taking care of themselves, etc. Have the students describe what they see in the pictures. Ask, "Why is taking care of ourselves important if we want peace?" Stress this: Peace starts with the individual. Tell the students that when they take care of themselves, they are meeting their physical, emotional, and safety needs. Ask, "How do you feel when your needs are not met?" Guide students to see that when their needs are not met, they do not feel peaceful inside.

8. Show pictures depicting results of not taking care of yourself, one another, and the earth. Have students describe and discuss. Encourage full participation.

9. Ask students to draw or write about a time when they have taken care of themselves, someone else, or the environment. Have them share their pictures and stories. Allow time for discussion. Thank each child who shares.

10. Ask, "Where does peace start?" Guide the children to reiterate that peace starts with the individual. Have the children work in small groups, each child writing or drawing his or her own definition or idea of peace. Explain that the way they work together can be a peacemaking activity. Ask, "How can we be peaceful as we work together?" Encourage the sharing of ideas.

11. Have the children read or show their definitions or pictures of what they interpret peace to be. Discuss. Hang the pictures on the bulletin board, and enjoy them. Each time you need some extra peacefulness inside, look at the pictures.

PEACE MEANS TAKING CARE OF OURSELVES, EACH OTHER, & OUR EARTH

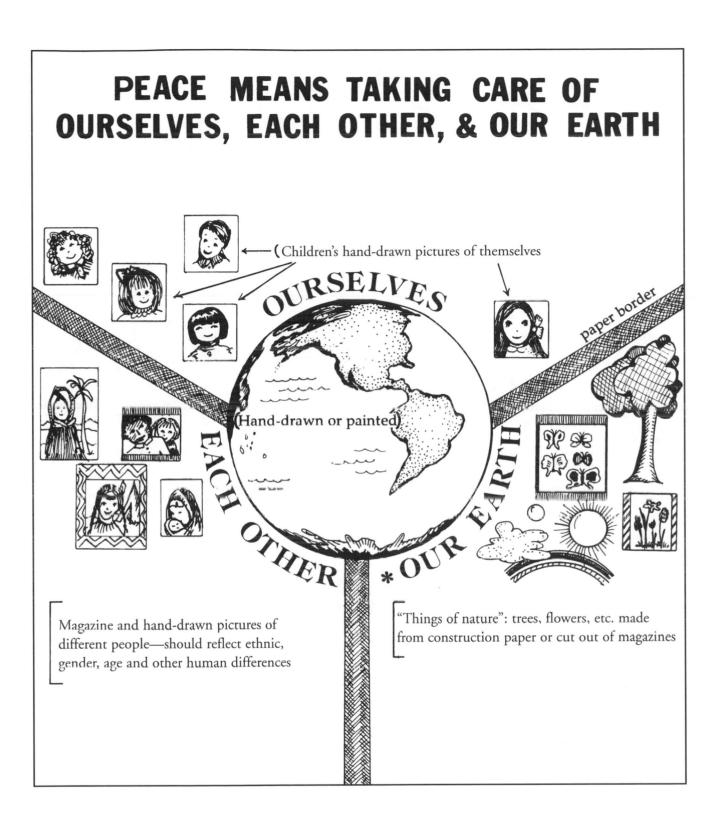

(Children's hand-drawn pictures of themselves

OURSELVES

paper border

(Hand-drawn or painted)

EACH OTHER

*OUR EARTH

Magazine and hand-drawn pictures of different people—should reflect ethnic, gender, age and other human differences

"Things of nature": trees, flowers, etc. made from construction paper or cut out of magazines

LESSON *6*

All Grades

The Process of Affirming

Objectives

- The children will understand that peace starts with the individual, and when they affirm others they create an atmosphere of acceptance that is crucial to peacemaking.
- The children will understand and use the process of affirmation in school and at home.

Materials

- Poem: "Being Human Is Being Special" (page 135)
- "The Process of Affirming" Poster:
- Paper and pencils for kids old enough to express themselves through writing; crayons and drawing paper for younger children

The Process of Affirming

- First, just notice what is special about the other person.
- Make a sincere statement to the other person about whatever is positive or special about him/her.
- Be sure to look directly at the other person as you speak.

- Relax, and know that the other person is just like you inside.

Procedure

1. Ask the class to sit in a circle.
2. Read the poem "Being Human Is Being Special."
3. State, "Each of you is very special. I like being your teacher. I think you're great." Pause and look at your students. Ask them how they felt when you just spoke the words you did. Tell them that what you just did was to affirm them. Say, "When we affirm, we make a sincere, positive statement about another person or people."
4. Ask, "How do you feel when people affirm you?" Discuss. Don't be surprised if some students express feelings of embarrassment and awkwardness at being acknowledged. This is natural.
5. Refer to the poster: The Process of Affirming. Read it to the class. Remind the class that peace begins with each of us. When we affirm one another it creates an atmosphere of acceptance that is crucial to peacemaking. Say, "When we feel accepted by other people

it becomes easier to work out our differences with them. We're all the same inside, but sometimes we forget that. Affirming helps connect us in a special way. Today we're going to learn to affirm one another. We can affirm people any time at all. The more we concentrate on the positive things about people, the easier it is to get along."

6. State, "Now we're going to have the opportunity to affirm one another in pairs. This is especially important if your partner is someone you don't usually 'hang around' with. Remember that not having peace often results from not accepting people who are different from us in some way. Boys and girls not accepting one another is a perfect example of this. How many boys in here have felt negatively toward another person because that person happens to be a girl?" Ask for a show of hands. "How many girls have had negative feelings toward others because those people happen to be boys?" Ask for a show of hands.

7. Say, "Peace starts with the individual and it starts with the daily decisions we make about other people. If we're committed to being peacemakers, then we must decide to focus more on likenesses than differences. We need to remember our commitment to peace even when we are faced with barriers." Explain the meaning of barriers.

8. Say, "How you will have an opportunity to overcome a barrier, to be a peacemaker, and to affirm someone else—even if that person isn't someone you normally play with."

9. Say, "Turn and face the person who is sitting next to you. Each person should have a partner. Acknowledge that person by nodding your head. Remember that any negative faces or comments you might make are a put-down to that person. Be kind."

10. Say, "Now let's all take a deep breath and get very calm and relaxed. Let any negative thoughts leave you. If they come back just let them pass. Just look at the person you're sitting across from. Notice that this person has eyes, nose, mouth and hair—just like you. Realize that this person has a brain and a heart beating inside—just like you. Know that this person has the same need for love and acceptance that you have."

11. Say, "Now think of something positive about your partner. Is it his or her smile, or eyes, or is it something about the way this person acts that's positive? Affirm your partner, stating the positive quality you thought of." Allow time for the partners to affirm one another. Some might need coaching from the teacher. Every student should be encouraged to complete the affirmation.

12. Have the students face front in a circle. Ask, "How did you feel during this activity?" Discuss. Allow the feelings of awkwardness to surface, especially in older children. Encourage their honesty and candor. Affirm them for participating.

13. Now state, "I am going to affirm each of you." Go around the circle and say something positive to each child. Be careful to notice your own barriers. If you're comfortable, shake hands, or put your hand on an arm or shoulder as you speak.

NOTE: When I did this with my class, I held both hands as I spoke to each child. It was very moving; in fact, I had to blink back tears as I looked deeply into the eyes of each of my students. A strong feeling of warmth and care connected us. It was a special moment that brought us all closer together.

14. If there's time, repeat the process with the same partners. Say, "Let's affirm our partners again." Restate the importance of affirming others. Ask the students to affirm someone when they go home.

15. Ask each student to draw an "affirmation picture" of their partner. This picture

should reflect the positive quality they noticed in that person. Below the picture, older children can write the affirmation too. Example: "Billy is kind. He shares his eraser with me."

NOTE: Depending on your class and the age of your students, you can expand affirmations to include handshaking and hugs. In my class, it eventually became very normal to see children hug one another. A wonderful experience arose out of a conflict between two of my "tough" little boys. One child asked me to mediate a conflict. I asked if he would go back to the child with whom he was having the conflict, work it out, and then affirm one another. In time I noticed the two boys talking, then shaking hands, and eventually hugging.

BEING HUMAN IS BEING SPECIAL

by Naomi Drew

I look in the mirror and who do I see.
My very own person who looks just like me.
I look at my eyes, I look at my face,
Knowing that no one on earth or in space
Is quite like I am, one of a kind.
My body is special and so is my mind.
Each person alive has something special to give.
We each make a difference each day that we live.
I love myself and I love others too.
The world is a special place,
'Cause it has me and you.

Grades 2-6

Dealing With Feelings

Objectives

By the end of this lesson students will be able to—
1. Identify a large variety of feelings and have some understanding of each.
2. Understand that everyone has feelings.
3. Move in the direction of greater self-acceptance.
4. Understand that we must choose our actions wisely and with conscience, particularly in the face of anger.

Materials

1. Charts:

| Feelings are neither right nor wrong, they just *are*. |

| Notice your feelings and choose your actions wisely. |

2. Large mural paper for a "feelings collage."
3. Chart paper for brainstorming chart.
4. Glue, scissors, markers, crayons.
5. Chalkboard, chalk.

  NOTE: The day before doing this lesson, assign the following homework. Cut out pictures and words that depict feelings. You can also include pictures of things that bring out certain feelings in you (joy, sorrow, dread). These pictures will be used to create a class collage.

Procedure

(This lesson can be carried over two days.)

1. Divide the class into small groups, asking each group to brainstorm as many kinds of feelings as they can. Allow students to use the dictionary, thesaurus, and the pictures/words they have cut out for homework. Each group should compile a list of ten to fifteen feelings. Before brainstorming, you can do the following brief warm-up. Say:
 • You're going to have a test tomorrow. How do you feel?
 • Someone criticizes your clothes in front of the class. How do you feel?
 • Your mother says that you can stay home from school tomorrow and do anything you want. How do you feel?
 • You forgot to bring an important assignment to school. How do you feel?
 • You find out you passed a test you thought you had failed. How do you feel?

Allow the class to discuss these feelings briefly and other feelings mentioned by the children prior to brainstorming.

2. Now have the groups brainstorm for 5-10 minutes; then, share their lists with the class. Record the feelings they come up with on the brainstorming chart.

3. Next have the class glue the pictures/words they brought in for homework on the chart paper to create a "feelings collage." They can write "feeling words" all over the chart in different colored markers. They can intersperse original drawings as well.

4. Have the class look at the collage when it is complete and list any other feelings they can think of for the brainstorming chart. Discuss.

5. Now show the poster, "Feelings are neither right nor wrong, they just are." Discuss this idea. Reinforce the notions that (1) all people have feelings and (2) feelings are part of what makes us human.

6. Now refer to the chart, "Notice your feelings and choose your actions wisely."

   Discuss, emphasizing that we all have the capacity to choose our actions, even in the face of uncomfortable or difficult emotions. Give a personal example.

7. Bring up the idea of anger, and how we especially have to make responsible choices in the face of anger. Talk about how cooling off enables us to put some distance between our feelings (anger) and the people and/or situations that cause it. Remind the class of the importance of separating anger from its cause if we want to have a peaceful school, home, neighborhood, or world. End the lesson by emphasizing that peace starts with each of us. One way a person can contribute to a peaceful world is by choosing his or her actions wisely.

Homework

Have students write in their journals about the last time they were engaged in conflict. Ask them to identify and write about their feelings at the time of the conflict and the actions they took. Next have them write about actions they might choose to take should a similar conflict occur in the future. Tomorrow, have the class discuss their journals.

Grades 2-6

Reflective Listening With Conflicts

Objectives

By the end of this lesson students will be able to—

1. Understand how to listen in conflict situations.
2. Practice role-playing reflective listening in conflict situations.

Materials

1. Role-play papers (see page 141).
2. Chalkboard, chalk.
3. Definition of reflective listening (see #2) on a chart.
4. Chart papers, markers.

Procedure

1. On the board write the words "Good Listening." Ask, "What does this mean? What is good listening?" Allow the children time to define the elements of good listening.
2. Say, "Today I'm going to show you how to take good listening a step further." Show the following definition.

> Reflective listening means listen to the other person with an open mind and then saying back or paraphrasing what you heard.

3. Demonstrate reflective listening by saying to a child, "Tell me about your favorite after-school activity." As the child speaks, look directly at him or her, nod from time to time, don't interrupt, and keep your full focus on what the child is saying. When the child finishes speaking paraphrase what he or she has said, starting with "I heard you say. . . ." When you're finished, ask the child if you paraphrased what he or she said correctly.
4. Ask the class, "What did you notice about the way I listened to _____?" Try to elicit from the students the elements referred to in step 3. List each point on chart paper and give prompts if necessary.
5. Ask the person you just listened to, "How did you feel when I listened to you that way?" Discuss the child's response.
6. Say, "When people listen to each other in the way you just observed, it helps them get along better. Then if a conflict arises, it's easier to work it out."

7. Ask, "How many people listen in the way I just demonstrated?" Discuss. "Now let's take a look at the way many people listen." (Have fun with this part). Ask for a volunteer. Have the child come to the front of the room. "Say, tell me all about your favorite book." As the child answers, look around the room, play with your hair, straighten your clothes, and whisper to someone else. Then interrupt the person speaking and start talking about your favorite book.

8. Now ask, "How was my listening different from before?" Ask the child who volunteered to tell the class how it felt to be listened to in this way. Have the class specify the differences between good listening and bad listening from these examples.

9. Say, "Now let's try some good listening together." Review the qualities of good listening; then on the board, write the question, "What is your favorite thing to do after school?" Divide the students into pairs. Have each pair take turns asking each other the question and listening reflectively while the other speaks. Before they begin, tell them that they can start their reflective listening statements with the words, "I heard you say . . . ."

10. Briefly discuss the interaction with the class. Say, "Now we're going to try the same technique with conflict situations." Distribute the conflict role-plays (paper strips) to each pair of children after you demonstrate one in front of the class. Remind students to use "I messages" when stating each problem. For example, "I'm annoyed that you took my pencil."

11. Have one partner state the problem on the first role-play paper, while the other partner listens and reflects what is heard. Then have the speaker and listener switch roles for each new role-play (three more).

12. Circulate as the children role-play, giving help where needed.

13. After about ten minutes, discuss with the class the interaction of each pair of children.

Homework

Have the students practice reflective listening with someone at school or home. Have them write in their journals describing how the people responded and what resulted from the interaction (e.g., good feelings, solution to a problem). Ask them to explain (in writing) how being a good listener can help them in their lives.

Conflict Role Plays

Copy this page and cut into strips. Distribute four role-play strips to each pair of children.)	• Someone you know doesn't invite you to a party but invites all the other kids in your group.
• Your friend takes the pencil you just dropped on the floor and starts using it. Now you have no pencil.	• A kid makes fun of you in the lunchroom.
• The student behind you in line bumps into you and doesn't say "Excuse me."	• A girl you know talks about you "behind your back."
• Your best friend starts hanging out with someone else and doesn't include you.	• The boy you sit next to accuses you of cheating. (You're not cheating.)
• Your mother yells at you because you haven't cleaned your room in a week.	• A good friend ignores you on the playground.
• A classmate is sarcastic to you in front of the class. You feel embarrassed.	• The person who sits across from you makes fun of your new sneakers.
• The person you're working with on a project rips your paper accidentally.	• In the lunchroom, someone looks at your sandwich and makes a face.
• Your friend promises to return your book in the morning but forgets it. You're angry because you really need that book.	• As you walk down the hall by yourself, two kids standing on the side seem to be laughing at you.

LESSON *9*

Grades 2-6

Exploring the Issue of Stereotypes

Objectives

By the end of this lesson students will be able to—

1. Understand the meaning of the words "stereotype" and "prejudice."
2. Become more aware of stereotypes and prejudices in our world.
3. Gain awareness that stereotyping others and exercising prejudice are negative practices that we should avoid.

Materials

1. Story: *Amazing Grace* by Mary Hoffman.
2. Chalkboard, chalk.

Procedure

1. On the chalkboard, write this definition/ explanation of stereotypes:

   A stereotype is a belief that people of a certain group are all the same and share identical negative traits. People who believe stereotypes don't understand that each person is *unique* ("unlike any other," "one of a kind").

Give the following examples: Some people believe that girls aren't as good in sports as boys. Others believe boys aren't as good in writing as girls. Say, "These beliefs simply aren't true. They imply that every girl 'is a certain way, ' (as athletes all girls are alike) and that every boy is 'a certain way, too (as writers all boys are alike)." Discuss.

2. Say, "Some people learn stereotypes from their families, without ever questioning what they believe. Can you think of any stereotypes you've read about or heard about?" Discuss. Ask, "Are stereotypes fair? Discuss.

3. Write the word "prejudice" on the chalkboard. Say, " Prejudice often result from stereotypes. 'Prejudice' is a hatred or suspicion of another race, religion, color, gender, or ethnic group— people who appear or seem different from you. Can you think of any examples of prejudice?" Guide the children to look at the issues of slavery and civil rights. Refer to the work of Martin Luther King, Jr.

4. Say, "Peacemakers don't practice prejudice or stereotyping. Do you know why? Discuss.

5. Tell the children that you're going to read them a story that addresses the issue of stereotyping. Say, "At the end of this story

I'd like you to tell me what stereotypes were present."

6. Read *Amazing Grace*. Ask what stereotypes the children noticed in the story and how they were addressed. Ask what lesson the story contains. Ask why all people should be treated as individuals? Discuss the children's responses.

Homework

Have the children write in their journals what they now understand about stereotypes and prejudice. Say, "Tomorrow we're going to participate in a day-long activity where you'll be personally involved in these issues."

Grades 2-6

Group Simulation: Exploring Stereotypes and Prejudice

Objectives

By the end of this lesson the children will be able to—

1. Understand how stereotypes can create prejudice.
2. Understand what it feels like to be stereotyped.
3. Understand that we need to accept people we perceive as different and not judge their differences negatively.

Materials

1. 2 × 2 yellow tags to be worn by half the children in your class.
2. 2 × 2 green tags to be worn by half the children in your class.
3. Safety pins.
4. Several pieces of chart paper and markers.
5. *The Story of Ruby Bridges* by Robert Coles.
6. Stereotyping sheets. Each member of the green group gets a green tag with the following statements written on it:

You can't trust people with yellow tags.
They aren't smart and don't tell the truth.
And, they have weird hair.

Each member of the yellow group gets a yellow tag with the following message written on it:

You can't trust people with green tags.
They think they're smart and they steal.
And, they're sloppy looking.

Procedure

1. First thing in the morning divide your class into two groups of mixed gender and ethnicity. Try to separate all good friends. Pin the yellow tags on one group; the green tags on the other group.
2. Say, "All day we're going to pretend that we have two distinctly different groups in our class. Each group will get a sheet that describes the stereotypes of the other group. You will not see the papers that tell about your own group. You are going to see what it's like to live with prejudice.

   Children in the green group are not allowed to be friends with the children in the yellow group. Don't help each other in any way. All day I want you to act as though you believe the stereotypes on your sheet. Later today you will get to take off your tags and be friends again; but until then, I want you to take your tags very seriously. There's an important lesson in it for you. Any questions?"

3. Have the groups go to opposite ends of the room. Distribute the stereotype sheets. Tell the groups they may gossip about each other.

4. Say: "Now we're going to go about our routines. Pretend that you are prejudiced against the other group. Act accordingly."

   NOTE: Teach your usual lessons all morning. Try not to stop unless the activity gets out of hand. Have the children go to lunch and recess with their tags on, and encourage them to keep up the simulation. You can have the children take off their tags after lunch or at the end of the day, just so you can allow time for debriefing.

5. After the children have taken off their tags, say, "What was that like for you?" Don't rush; elicit responses from as many people as possible.

6. Ask, "What did you learn about stereotypes and prejudice? Discuss. List insights on chart paper.

7. Were you able to tell what stereotypes the other group believed about you from the way they acted? Discuss.

8. Ask, "How can we help rid the world of prejudice?" List on chart paper.

9. Close by reading *The Story of Ruby Bridges*, by Robert Coles.

Homework

Write about your experiences today and what new insights you gained about stereotypes and prejudice. Tomorrow make time to discuss these insights.

Grades 2-6

How Are We The Same, How Are We Different?

Objectives

By the end of this lesson, students will be able to—

1. Understand that we are all have similar to and different from each other..
2. Have a greater awareness of our similarities.
3. Have greater sensitivity toward others.
4. Understand what they can do to promote acceptance of diversity.

Materials

1. Chart paper (3 sheets), markers.
2. Chairs in a circle, one for each member of the class.
3. For follow-up tomorrow: mural paper, glue, pictures showing differences that children cut from magazines at home.

Procedure

1. Say, "All people are alike in some ways, different in other ways. Today we're going to play a game that will help you focus on likenesses. It's called 'I'm Looking For.' In this game you will sit in a circle, and one person will begin by saying, 'I'm looking for _____,' filling in the blank with something like 'people wearing red shirts.' Everyone wearing a red shirt then gets up and walks around the inside of the circle and one chair is removed. After all children have walked around for a minute or two, the person in the middle yells, 'Sit,' and they all have to find a chair. The person who is left without a chair goes to the middle and says, 'I'm looking for_____,' and fills in the blank with something else. You can focus on types of clothing, birthday months, hair color, types of families, favorite holidays, favorite foods, or other things the children can relate to.

2. Play the game. At the end, ask, "How many of you found that you had something in common with other members of the class. What were some of the things you had in common? Discuss, eliciting as many commonalities as possible.

3. At the top of a sheet of chart paper, write, "Ways People Are Alike." Ask the children to think about all the people in the world. Say, "In what ways do you think everyone in the world is alike; what common characteristics do we share?" On the chart, list as many characteristics as you can. Prompt the

children to think of emotional and physical needs that all human beings have (food, shelter, love, respect). Ask if they think kids in other parts of the world have needs similar to their own.

4. Ask the children to think about the members of the class and the school. Ask if they believe the needs among them are similar? Discuss.

5. Say, "Sometimes in our world people form prejudices because they look too much at differences and not enough at similarities." Ask, "What can we do about this?" Discuss.

6. On another chart paper write, "Ways We Can See Beyond Differences." Encourage the children to come up with concrete things they can do to see similarities in people beyond the apparent differences. **B**rainstorming groups may be used to generate a list. Joint responses should be listed on the chart at the end of the brainstorming session.

7. Remind the children that conflicts often arise because of perceived differences, So to be peacemakers, we must focus on our commonalities instead.

Homework

Have the children write in their journals about what they learned from today's lesson. Also, have each child write what he or she will do to promote acceptance of others.

Follow-up

Have the children cut out magazine pictures of different kinds of people. Tomorrow, have them glue the chart (Ways We Are All Alike) into the middle of a large sheet of mural paper. Then, glue the pictures around the chart. Culminate by asking the children to share and discuss their journal entries.

Glossary

bias   prejudice

conflict resolution   the strategies needed for working out a conflict

discrimination   an act based on prejudice

diversity   the differences among people; variety

ethnic group   people classed according to common racial, national, or cultural background

gender   being either male or female

I message   a declarative sentence starting with "I" that expresses a feeling or position; the opposite of a you message," e.g., I feel angry" as opposed to You make me angry."

majority   the larger or main group of people in a population or the group that possesses the greatest power; e.g., white males in the corporate work force

minority   the smaller of two groups of people that make up a total population

peer mediation   the act of helping another person or people resolve a dispute

prejudice   a judgment or opinion held in disregard of facts; unreasonable biases that are usually negative; intolerance of another race, religion, color, gender, or ethnic group

race   a family, group, people, or nation of the same background

reflective listening   careful listening to another person followed by paraphrasing what is said/heard

stereotype   a belief that all members of a certain group of people are exactly the same in their sharing of identical traits; e.g., all girls are bad at sports; blonds have more fun

Tips for Parents

- Start the practice of family meetings. Encourage your child to tell you what he or she learned about the process of creating a peaceful classroom. Create guidelines with your family for a peaceful home. Ask each member of your household to describe a peaceful home in detail. Ask how you need to treat each other to have a peaceful atmosphere in your home. List each person's suggestions and hang the list on the refrigerator. Add a title: Our Guidelines for a Peaceful Home. Expect each member to honor these "family standards.".

- *Make your home a put-down free zone.* Starting today make a promise to yourself never to use put-downs of any kind. Model this for your children, and ask them to do the same.

- *Practice using "I messages." Teach your entire family how to do them.* Communicate respectfully but assertively. Read Thomas Gordon's *P.E.T, Parent Effectiveness Training* to help with this aim

- *Post the Win/Win Guidelines in your home.* Use them with your children, spouse, others in your home, and friends. Make a commitment

to resolve conflicts peacefully. Read *Teaching Children Self-Discipline At Home and At School* by Thomas Gordon for more details on peaceful resolution of conflicts.

- When conflicts arise, avoid doing the six things that make them worse:
  - threatening
  - preaching
  - judging
  - comparing
  - blaming
  - name-calling

  Read *How to Talk So Kids Will Listen* and *Listen So Kids Will Talk* by Adele Faber and Elaine Mazlish for comprehensive details.

- Set fair, consistent limits for your children, along with reasonable consequences for surpassing them. Try to avoid spanking.

- Listen to your child with all your heart. Practice and model good listening at all times. Read *Your Child's Self-Esteem* by Dorothy Corkille Briggs to learn more about good listening and other methods of fostering high self-image in children.

- Teach your children to be ethical people. Children learn by example. We need to help them be honest people who show respect for others. Read *The Moral Intelligence of Children* by Robert Coles for insightful information in this area.

- Read and discuss peacemaking-related storybooks your child has been introduced to in class. Let your child tell you what important lessons he or she learned and how these lessons can be applied in the home. Use the bibliography at the end of this book to find other peacemaking-related literature to read and talk about with your child.

- Be a "peacemaking" role model for your children. Cool off when angry; treat others with kindness and respect; show tolerance toward people who are different; show care for the world and the people in it, and put your highest beliefs into action.

- Be forgiving and compassionate. Teach your children to do the same.

- Get in touch with this organization for excellent parenting materials:
  Parenting for Peace and Justice Network
  c/o The Institute for Peace and Justice
  4144 Lindell, Suite 408
  St. Louis, MO 63108

The Effects of Peacemaking on Children Over Time

How does peacemaking affect children who have been taught these skills for three, four, and give years? What follows are the words of some fourth and fifth grade students who have been learning and practicing peacemaking since they were in kindergarten and first grade. Their experiences are representative of many other children who have had the good fortune of learning these skills at an early age.

Gianna, Grade 4: "I always use peacemaking if I am not agreeing with someone. For instance, if someone says something that hurts my feelings, I walk away to cool off. Then I come back to speak to that person, and tell them, 'I don't like it when you say that to me.' The other person then says something back to me, showing that he or she understands my feelings. We brainstorm solutions so this problem doesn't happen again. Peacemaking is the best way to get along with others."

Curtis, Grade 5: "Peacemaking has affected me since first grade. I remember thinking peacemaking was just for *dorks*, but now all of that has changed. I think peacemaking is for intelligent, smart, cool people. It helps you work out conflicts so you can go on being friends. Another every important part is affirmations. If you have a goal in life, you have to think you can do it. Say, 'I can do this' over and over again, until you finally can. That's an important way to achieve your goal. You can achieve anything."

Vikram, Grade 4: "Peacemaking means a lot of things, but mainly it means to resolve your conflicts with other people. Peacemaking is simple through the Win/Win Guidelines. I use every step whenever I have a problem."

Elizabeth, Grade 5: "Peacemaking helps me because I use the Win/Win Guidelines with my brother and we always feel better. Afterwards we feel as if we never fought. When I first used win/win I wasn't sure if it would work or not. Now I know for sure and I try to get other people to use it with me all the time."

Sandra: "Peacemaking has made me a better and nicer person. I have more friends and I don't get into fights. I help people out when they need it and I use the Win/Win Guidelines."

Nina: "I wanted to help kids solve problems so I became a peer mediator. It makes me feel better, and it's a good way to solve problems instead of fighting."

Collin, Grade 4: "I use peacemaking all the time for a lot of different things, like when people start to push, shove, and curse. I use it when other people or myself get in a fight or argument. I also use it at home, when my sister takes something without asking, or when we decide who gets what, and when we switch toys or anything like that. If I didn't have the steps of peacemaking what would help meet figure out problems?"

Concluding Thoughts

Nothing is more powerful than an individual acting out of his own conscience, thus bringing the collective conscience to life.

Norman Cousins

The role of teacher encompasses much more than academics. Teachers have the ability to touch the hearts and consciences of students along with their intellects.

Excellent teachers can be powerful role models, inspiring students toward greater dignity, compassion, and success. The work we do as teachers is transformational. In other words, we shape lives.

By teaching children to respect themselves and others, resolve conflicts nonviolently, communicate effectively, and take responsibility for their actions, teachers assist them in building a positive

future, for themselves and the rest of the world. Teaching is indeed a tremendous challenge, yet along with the challenge is an extraordinary opportunity to affect the whole world. After all, teachers have as their daily work the job of crafting hearts and minds.

We also have the opportunity to provide children with an alternative reality, one where compassion and dignity are standards, where each person is held accountable for his or her words and actions and where peace and equality are possible. As we do so, we move closer to the ideal defined by writer and educator Vivian Gussin Paley, who said, ". . . our ultimate goal as teachers in a democratic society [is] helping children become kind and caring participants in a world that includes everyone." (*Starting Small*, iii)

Decades ago Martin Luther King, Jr. wrote, "I suggest that the philosophy and strategy of nonviolence become immediately the subject for study and for serious experimentation in every field of human conflict." What better way to keep his dream alive than to begin in our public schools, one teacher and one child at a time.

Bibliography

Books for Adults

Akin, Terry and Palomares, Susanna. *Managing Conflict.* Torrance, CA: Innerchoice Publishing, 1995.

Ashton-Warner, Sylvia. *Teacher.* New York: Touchstone, 1963.

Beach, Richard. *A Teacher's Introduction to Reader-Response Theories.* Urbana, IL: NCTE, 1993.

Bickmore, K. *Alternatives to Violence.* Alternatives To Violence Committee, 1984.

Bissex, Glenda and Bullock, Richard (ed.). *Seeing for Ourselves.* Portsmouth, NH: Heinemann, 1987.

Breathnach, Sarah Ban. *Simple Abundance.* New York: Warner Books, 1995.

Briggs, Dorothy Corkille. *Celebrate Yourself.* New York: Doubleday, 1977.

Briggs, Dorothy Corkille. *Your Child's Self-Esteem.* New York: Doubleday, 1975.

Bruner, Jerome. *The Process of Education.* Cambridge, MA: Harvard University Press, 1977.

Calkins, Lucy McCormick. *The Art of Teaching Writing* (new edition). Portsmouth, NH: Heinemann, 1994.

Chopra, Deepak. *The Seven Spiritual Laws of Success.* San Rafael, CA: New World Library, 1994.

Coles, Robert. *The Call of Stories.* Boston: Houghton Mifflin, 1989.

Cornelius, H. and Faire, S. *Everyone Can Win.* New York: Simon & Schuster, 1993.

Cousins, Norman. *Human Options.* New York: Norton & Co., 1981.

Cowan, David. *Taking Charge of Organizational Conflict.* Torrance, CA: Innerchoice Publishing, 1995.

Cowan, D. Palomares, S. and Schilling, D. *Conflict Resolution Skills for Teens.* Torrance, CA: Innerchoice Publishing, 1994.

Cowan, D. Palomares, S. and Schilling, D. *Teaching the Skills of Conflict Resolution.* Torrance, CA: Innerchoice Publishing, 1992.

Drew, N. *Learning the Skills Of Peacemaking.* Torrance, CA: Jalmar Press, 1995.

Dryden, Gordon and Vos, Jeannette. *The Learning Revolution.* Torrance, CA: Jalmar Press, 1994.

Dunne, Gerry. *Preventing Violence in Our Schools.* Torrance, CA: Jalmar Press, 1999.

Dyer, Wayne. *Your Erroneous Zones.* New York: HarperCollins Publishers, 1976.

Dyson, Anne Haas and Genishi, Cecilia (editors). *The Need for Story: Cultural Diversity in Classroom and Community.* Urbana, IL: NCTE, 1994.

Dyson, Anne Haas. *Social Worlds of Children Learning to Write in an Urban Primary School.* New York: Teachers College Press, 1993.

Educators for Social Responsibility. *Perspectives.* Cambridge, MA: ESR, 1983.

Elbow, Peter. *Writing with Power.* New York: Oxford University Press, 1981.

Elbow, Peter. *Embracing Contraries.* New York: Oxford University Press, 1986.

Faigley, Lester. *Fragments of Rationality.* Pittsburgh, PA, University of Pittsburgh Press, 1992.

Faber Adele and Mazlish, Elaine. *How To Talk So Kids Can Learn.* New York: Fireside, 1995.

Frankl, Victor. *Man's Search for Meaning.* Boston: Beacon Press.

Freire, Paulo. *Pedagogy of the Oppressed.* New York: Continuum, 1983.

Friere, Paulo. *Education for Critical Consciousness.* New York: Continuum, 1994.

Friere, Paulo. *Pedagogy of Hope.* New York: Continuum, 1995.

Fromm, Erich. *Escape from Freedom.* New York: Holt, Henry & Co., Inc. 1960.

Gardner, Howard. *The Unschooled Mind.* New York: Basic Books, 1991.

Glasser, William. *Schools Without Failure.* New York: Harper and Row, 1969.

Goleman, Daniel. *Emotional Intelligence*. New York: Bantam Books, 1995.

Gordon, Thomas, *P.E.T. Parent Effectiveness Training*. New York: Plume, 1975.

Gordon, Thomas. *Teaching Children Self-Discipline*. New York: Random House, 1989.

Hanh, Thich Nhat. *Peace Is Every Step*. New York: Bantam Books, 1992.

Heard, Georgia. *Writing Toward Home*. Portsmouth, NH: Heinemann, 1995.

Heard, Georgia. *For the Good of the Earth and the Sun*. Portsmouth, NH: Heinemann, 1989.

Hill, Bonnie; Johnson, Nancy; and Noe, Katherine Schlick. *Literature Circles and Response*. Norwood, MA: Christopher-Gordon, 1995.

Holly, Mary Louise. *Writing to Grow*. Portsmouth, NH: Heinemann, 1987.

Hubbard, Ruth Shagoury and Power, Brenda Miller. *The Art of Classroom Inquiry*. Portsmouth, NH: Heinemann, 1993.

Johnson, David and Johnson, Roger. *Teaching Students To Be Peacemakers*. Interaction Book Co., 1991.

Johnson, Spencer. *One Minute for Myself*. New York: William Morrow, 1985.

Kabat-Zinn, John. *Wherever You Go, There You Are*. New York: Hyperion, 1994.

Kabattchenko, M. et al. *Peace in 100 Languages*. Torrance, CA: Jalmar Press, 1999.

Kilpatrick, William. *Why Johnny Can't Tell Right from Wrong*, New York: Touchstone, 1993.

Knoblauch, C.H. and Brannon, Lil. *Critical Teaching and the Idea of Literacy*. Portsmouth, NH: Heinemann, 1993.

Knowles, Horace (ed.) *A Treasury of American Writers from Harper's Magazine*. New York: Bonanza Books, 1985.

Kramer, Patricia and Frazer, Linda. *The Dynamics of Relationships*. Kensington, MD: Equal Partners, 1990.

Kreidler, William. *Creative Conflict Resolution*. Glenview, IL: Scott Foresman, 1984.

Likona, Thomas: *Educating for Character*. New York: Bantam Books, 1991.

Macy, Joanna Rogers. *Despair and Personal Power in the Nuclear Age*. Philadelphia: New Society, 1983.

Norton, Donna. *Through the Eyes of a Child*. Englewood Cliffs, NJ: Merrill (Division of Simon & Schuster), 1993.

O'Reilley, Mary Rose. *The Peaceable Classroom*. Portsmouth, NH: Heinemann, 1994.

Piaget, Jean. "Intelligence and Affectivity: Their Relationship During Child Development" in *Annual Reviews*. Palo Alto, CA.: 1981.

Peck, M. Scott. *A World Waiting To Be Born*. New York: Bantam Books, 1994.

Prutzman, Priscilla and others. *The Friendly Classroom for a Small Planet*. Nyack, NY: Avery Publishing.

Ramsey, Patricia, *Teaching and Learning in a Diverse World: Multicultural Education for Young Children*. Colchester, VT: Teachers College Press.

Rose, Mike. *Lives on the Boundary*. New York: Penguin, 1989.

Rosenblatt, Louise. *Literature as Exploration*. New York: MLA, 1976.

Rosenberg, Marshall. *Nonviolent Communication*. Delmar, CA: Puddle Dancer Press, 1999.

Routman, Reggie. *Transitions*. Portsmouth, NH: Heinemann, 1988.

Schilling, Diane. *Getting Along*. Torrance, CA: Innerchoice Publishing, 1993.

Schmidt, F. and Friedman, A. *Creative Conflict Solving for Kids*. Miami Beach: Peace Education Foundation, 1991.

Steele, Eden. *Peace Patrol*. Torrance, CA: Innerchoice Publishing, 1994.

"Teaching Tolerance." *Starting Small*. Montgomery, AL: Southern Poverty Law Center, 1997.

Vygotsky, Lev. *Mind in Society: The Development of Higher Psychological Processes*. Cambridge, MA: Harvard University Press. 1978.

Wadsworth, Barry J. *Foundations of Constructivism: Piaget's Theory of Cognitive and Affective Development*. Reading, MA: Longman, 1971.

Wright, Esther. *Good Morning, Class, I Love You*. Torrance, CA: Jalmar Press, 1989.

Ziglar, Zig. *Raising Positive Kids in a Negative World*. New York: Nelson, 1988.

Periodicals

Arbus, Judith, "Building a Successful School Conflict Resolution Program," *Primary Voices*, Nov. 1994.

Ayers, William. "Teaching Is an Act of Hope." *Teaching Tolerance* (Fall 1995): 23-25.

Foderaro, Lisa, "You Don't Have to Fight," *New York Times, Education Life*, Jan. 9, 1994.

Gilbert, Susan. "Child Deaths: Violence Rises as Accidents Fall." *New York Times*, June 11, 1996.

Johnson, David, "Teaching Students to be Peer Mediators," *Educational Leadership*, Sept. 1992.

Mundell, Sue, "Why Teach Peace?" *Christian Science Monitor*, Aug., 1988.

Valentine, Glenda. "It's How You Play the Game." *Teaching Tolerance* (Fall 1995): 59-63.

Children's Books

Asch, Frank. *The Earth and I*. New York: Harcourt Brace, 1994.

Andersen, Bethanne. *Seven Brave Women*. New York: Greenwillow Books, 1997.

Baker, B. *Digby and Kate*. New York: E. P. Dutton, 1988.

Brandenberg, F. *It's Not My Fault*. New York: Greenwillow Books, 1980.

Coles, Robert: *The Story of Ruby Bridges*. New York: Scholastic, 1995.

Cohen, B. *Molly's Pilgrim*. New York: Lothrop, Lee & Shepard, 1978.

Crary, E. *I'm Mad*. Seattle: Parenting Press, 1991.

de Paolo, T. *Oliver Button Is a Sissy*. New York: Harcourt Brace Jovanovich, 1979.

Dragonwagon, C. *I Hate My Brother Harry*. New York: Harper & Row, 1983.

Durrell, Ann, and Marilyn Sachs, editors. *The Big Book for Peace*. New York: Dutton, 1990.

Durrell, Ann, Jean Craighead George, and Katherine Patterson, editors. *The Big Book for Our Planet*. New York: Dutton, 1994.

Ernst, Lisa Campbell. *Zinnia and Dot*. New York, 1992.

Gerson, Mary-Joan (retold by). *Why the Sky is Far Away: A Nigerian Folktale*. Boston: Little, Brown, 1992.

Goffstein, M. B. *Natural History*. New York: Farrar-Straus-Giroux, 1979.

Greenfield, E. *Rosa Parks*. Thomas Y. Crowell Co., 1973.

Hamanaka, Sheila. *All the Colors of the Earth*. New York: Morrow Junior Books.

Hamanaka, Sheila. *Peace Crane*. New York: Morrow Junior Books, 1995.

Hoberman, M. *My Song Is Beautiful*. New York: Little, Brown and Co., 1994.

Hoffman, Mary. *Amazing Grace*. New York: Dial Books, 1991.

Hudson, Wade. *Pass It On: African-American Poetry for Children*. New York: Scholastic, 1993.

Kidd, D. *Onion Tears*. New York: Orchard Books, 1989.

Le Tord, Bijou. *Elephant Moon*. New York: Delacorte, 1993.

Leverich, K. *Best Enemies Again*. New York: Greenwillow Books 1991.

Lionni, Leo. *Tillie and the Wall*. New York: Knopf, 1989.

Lucas, E. *Peace on the Playground*. Danbury, CT: Franklin Watts 1991.

MacDonald, Margaret Read. *Peace Tales*. Northaven, CT: Linnet Books, 1993.

Millman, Dan. *The Secret of the Peaceful Warrior*. Tiburon, CA: Starseed Press, 1991.

Naylor, Phyllis Reynolds. *King of the Playground*. New York: Atheneum, 1991.

Pearson, S. *Molly Moves Out*. New York: The Dial Press, 1979.

Raschka, Chris. *Yo! Yes?*. New York: Orchard Books, 1993.

Robb, Laura, and Debra Lill. *Music and Drum: Voices of War and Peace, Hope and Dreams*. New York: Philomel, 1997.

Robinson, N. *Wendy and The Bullies*. Norwalk, CT: Hastings House (United Publishers Group), 1980.

Saltzman, David. *The Jester Has Lost His Jingle*. Palo Verdes Estates, CA: Jester, Inc., 1995. (This book can be ordered by calling 1-800-9-JESTER.)

Schimmel, Schim. *Children of the Earth Remember*. Minocqua, WI: NorthWord Press, 1997. (This book can be ordered by calling 1-800-356-4465.)

Schimmel, Schim. *Dear Children of the Earth*. Minocqua, WI: NorthWord Press, 1997. (This book can be ordered by calling 1-800-356-4465.)

Scholes, Katherine. *Peace Begins with You*. Boston: Little, Brown, 1990.

Seuss, Dr. *The Butter Battle Book*. New York: Random House, 1984.

Seuss, Dr. *The Lorax*. New York: Random House, 1971.

Simon, N. *I Speak English for My Mom*. Morton Grove, IL: Albert Whitman & Co., 1981.

Spier, Peter. *People*. New York: Doubleday.

Van Leeuwen, J. *Oliver Pig at School*. New York: Dial Books (Penguin USA), 1990.

Vigna, Judith. *Black Like Kyra, White Like Me*. Morton Grove, IL: Albert Whitman & Company.

Wahl, J. *The Animals' Peace Day*. New York: Crown Publishers, 1970.

Walker, A. *Finding the Green Stone*. New York: Harcourt Brace Jovanovich, 1991.

Williams, B. *So What If I'm a Sore Loser*. New York: Harcourt Brace Jovanovich, 1981.

Zolotow, C. *The Hating Book*. New York: Harper & Row, 1969.

Zolotow, C. *The Quarreling Book*. New York: Harper & Row, 1963.

Zolotow, C. *The Unfriendly Book*. New York: Harper & Row, 1975.

Records, Tapes, Plays, and Music

Arm in Arm by Jennings. (Songs available from Plank Road Publishing, P.O. Box 26627, Wauwatosa, WI 53226-0627. Telephone: 800-437-0832.)

American Heroes by Sprout. (Songs available from Sprout Recordings, P.O. Box 188, Morrisville, PA 19067. Telephone: 215-295-2726. Toll-free: 1-888-386-7664.)

Black & White by Jennings. (Songs available from Plank Road Publishing, P.O. Box 26627, Wauwatosa, WI 53226-0627. Telephone: 800-437-0832.)

Building Bridges original music and script. (Excellent song and play, highly recommended, available from Blue Sky Puppet Theater, 4301 Van Buren Street, University Park,MD 20782. Telephone: 301-927-5599.)

Celebrate You & Me by Emerson. (Musical available from J. W. Pepper. Telephone: 800-345-6296. FAX: 800-260-1482. Internet: http://www.jwpepper.com.)

Children of the World. (Available from Kimbo Educational, P.O. Box 477, Longbranch, NJ 07740. Telephone: 800-255-8629.)

Dona Nobis Pacem arr. by Jennings. (Songs available from Plank Road Publishing, P.O. Box 26627,Wauwatosa, WI 53226-0627. Telephone: 800-437-0832.)

Joining Hands with Other Lands. (Available from Kimbo Educational, P.O. Box 477, Longbranch, NJ 07740. Telephone: 800-255-8629.)

Kids are Kids the Whole World Round by Gemini and others. (Musical available from J. W. Pepper. Telephone: 800-345-6296. FAX: 800-260-1482. Internet: http:// www. jwpepper. com.)

Light the Candles All Around the World by Jennings. (Songs available from Plank Road Publishing, P.O. Box 26627, Wauwatosa, WI 53226-0627. Telephone: 800-437-0832.)

Lovin' Kindness by Gallina and Gallina. (Musical available from J. W. Pepper. Telephone: 800-345-6296. FAX: 800-260-1482. Internet: http://www.jwpepper.com.)

Lullabies for a New Age by Sprout. (Peaceful music for kids available from Sprout Recordings, P.O. Box 188, Morrisville, PA 19067. Telephone: 215-295-2726. Toll-free: 1-888-386-7664.)

Possibilities: A Celebration of Life by Jennings. (Musical available from Plank Road Publishing, P.O. Box 26627, Wauwatosa, WI 53226-0627. Telephone: 800-437-0832.)

Proud: A Celebration of Ourselves by Jennings. (Musical available from Plank Road Publishing, P.O. Box 26627, Wauwatosa, WI 53226-0627. Telephone: 800-437-0832.)

Put Your Hand in My Hand by Jennings. (Songs available from Plank Road Publishing, P.O. Box 26627, Wauwatosa, WI 53226-0627. Telephone: 800-437-0832.)

Songs for Peacemakers by Nass and Nass. (Cassette, video, and lessons available from Educational Activities, P.O. Box 392, Freeport, NY 11520. Telephone: 800-79-PEACE [800-797-3223].)

Teaching Peace by Grammer. (Cassette, songbook, and lessons [1993] available from Smilin' Atcha Music, Inc., P.O. Box 446, Chester, NY. Telephone 914-469-9450.)

Together: A Celebration of Our Global Community by Jennings. (Musical available from Plank Road Publishing, P.O. Box 26627, Wauwatosa, WI 53226-0627. Telephone: 800-437-0832.)

Two Hands Hold the Earth (Available from A Gentle Wind, P.O. Box 3103, Albany, NY 12201.)

We All Live Together. (Tape series available from Youngheart Records, Los Angeles, CA.)

We Share the Rainbow by Jennings. (Songs available from Plank Road Publishing, P.O. Box 26627, Wauwatosa, WI 53226-0627. Telephone: 800-437-0832.)

Where is the Peace by Jennings. (Songs available from Plank Road Publishing, P.O. Box 26627, Wauwatosa, WI 53226-0627. Telephone: 800-437-0832.)

You've Got the Power by Amorosia and Billingsley. (Musical available from J. W. Pepper. Telephone: 800-345-6296. FAX: 800-260-1482. Internet: http://www.jwpepper.com.)

ERRATA

Mea Culpa, Mea Culpa, Mea Maxima Culpa!

Somewhere between final editing, layout, design, and printing of this book, the most embarrassing thing that could happen to an educational materials publisher happened: A "Mistake Gremlin" floated in several punctuation and text errors. Ouch!

We assume full responsibility for the mistakes and will correct them in the next printing. However, we did want to respond to the demand for Naomi's newest book and felt the following mistakes did not affect the basic integrity of the book, so we made the decision to ship this book as is and to ask your indulgence in making the changes noted below in your personal copy of Peaceful Classroom in Action.

We note only spelling and other changes that could affect your best use of this book with your students. Punctuation errors are not specifically noted since they do not change the meaning of the material presented.

To "Thank You" for your understanding and for helping us get through our embarrassment, we are reducing the original price of this title from $24.95 to $14.95.

Page xvi	Line 8, left column	*xii* should read *xi*
Page xvi	Line 9, left column	*xv* should read *x*
Page 13	Line 28, left column	*See Page 0* should read *See page 14*
Page 21	Line 17, right column	*talkes* should read *talks*
Page 22	Line 24, left column	Insert *completely* between *conflicts* and *disappear*
Page 25	Line 12, right column	*he* should read *the*
Page 28	Line 4, left column	*I* should read *Am I*
Page 31	Line 9, right column	Insert *in* between *invest* and *showcasing*
Page 32	Line 24, right column	*get* should read *gets*
Page 32	Line 42, right column	*childrn* should read *children*
Page 36	Line 16, left column	Add a "." after *mad*
Page 41	Line 20, left column	*page 0* should read *page 12*
Page 44	Last Line, right column	*Fram* should read *Fran*
Page 46	Line 7, left column	*realize* should read *realized*
Page 46	Line 9, left column	*Teddy* should read *Teddy's*
Page 63	Line 27, right column	*Ben* should read *Ben's*
Page 66	Line 26, left column	Delete *(long quotation)*
Page 66	Line 29, right column	*October 3* should read *October 30*
Page 70	Line 3, right column	Insert *had* between *students* and *was*
Page 82	Line 32, right column	Insert *a* between *as* and *process*
Page 95	Line 3, right column	Replace *is* with *are*
Page 111	Line 20, right column	Insert *(page 112)* after *alone*
Page 116	Line 11, right column	*one* should read *on*
Page 123	Line 4, left column	*giving* should read *Giving*
Page 129	Line 10, left column	*(page 135)* should read *(page 132)*
Page 135	Line 8, left column	*(page 141)* should read *(page 137)*
Page 135	Line 10, left column	*(see #2)* should read *(see #2 under procedures)*
Page 135	Line 1, right column	*listen* should read *listening*
Page 141	Line 17, left column	*green tag* should read *a sheet*
Page 141	Line 22, left column	*yellow tag* should read *a sheet*
Page 143	Line 2, left column	Cross out *have*
Page 148	Line 2, left column	*give* should read *five*